# A DEEPER WELLNESS

## Conquering Stress, Mood, Anxiety, and Traumas

by Dr. Monica Vermani, C. Psych.

edited by Madonna M. McManus

A Deeper Wellness:  Conquering Stress, Mood, Anxiety, and Traumas

Copyright ©2022  Dr. Monica Vermani, C. Psych.

Published by VitaOdyssey Inc.


Paperback ISBN: 978-1-7779155-0-6
eISBN: 978-1-7779155-1-3

*This book is dedicated to you, as you strive to go deeper and become a higher, better version of yourself.*

## ACKNOWLEDGMENTS

I am deeply grateful for my wonderful family, who provide unstinting support for all that I take on, and love me just as I am. I thank my parents Om Parkash and Usha Vermani, who modeled courage, strength, and resilience as they navigated life's challenges as immigrants to Canada. They taught me, by example, to work hard and never give up. I thank my brother Sanjay and his wonderful wife Vicky with all my heart, and their twin daughters, my lovely nieces Tia and Maya. They have shown me how to reconnect with playfulness, love, laughter, healing, and the boundless joys of childhood.

A very special thank you to Dr. Giorgio Ilacqua, C. Psych., who encouraged me to become a clinical psychologist. When I began working for him as a psychometrist, he made out my first paycheque to Dr. Monica Vermani, a gesture that spoke volumes and ignited a passion that informed virtually every aspect of my career and my life. I would also like to acknowledge and thank the many clinicians who also believed in and supported me early in my career: Dr. Donna Ferguson, C. Psych., ABPP; Dr. David Nussbaum, PhD, Neuropsychologist; Dr. Martin Katzman, MD, FRCP(C), Psychiatrist; Dr. Lukasz Struzik, MD; Dr. Richard Brown, MD, Psychiatrist; and Dr. Pat Gerbarg, MD, Psychiatrist.

Special thanks to Andrea Olivera, Lorena Lasky, Paul Marhue, Raj Girn, Shelby Monita, Simone Purboo-Rennie, Paul Chato, Freedom Malhotra, Mario Lewis, Rev. Mark and Rev. Elaine Thomas, Rev. Cassandra Joan Butler, Marissa Eigenbrood, Janet Shapiro and Lydia Rasmussen of Smith Publicity, and Bethany Brown of The Cadence Group. My heartfelt gratitude and thanks to Sergio Lasky and Madonna McManus, who have believed in me from the start. They have worked endless hours to help manifest my goals.

Last — but not least — Rita DiLuca, Sandi Dwarka, Vinny Dwarka, Nam Do, Jessie Dimech, Ruth Davis, Milica Tempest, Christina Droumtsekas, Eyvonne Findlay, Margaret Bernat, Kaithy Wu, Rev. Sandra Atkinson, Laura Torrado, Olivia Blanchette, Julie Cummins-Chaudhari, Rev. Michelle Paterniti, Meena Tanna, Kiran Bedi-Ruparelia, Rohini and Paul Gill, Anita Bhandari, Angela and Jag Jodha, Vera Pavri, Margi Pagliaro, Monica Pagliaro-McInnis, Anju Virmani, Dr. Cheryl Bradbury, C. Psych., and Dr. Martha McKay, C. Psych., my closest friends who are also my family, who unstintingly love, support, encourage, and enrich my life. I am truly blessed with you all being a part of my life's journey. My sincere heartfelt love and gratitude to you all.

# TABLE OF CONTENTS

## A DEEPER WELLNESS

# FOREWORD

As Integrative Psychiatrists and mind-body teachers, it is a special honor to write the foreword to this book. We have known Dr. Monica Vermani for more than 20 years. Our work together began with a research study of the effects of a yoga breath intervention on people suffering from severe treatment-resistant anxiety and comorbid emotional disorders. Many of those who participated in the study were patients of Dr. Vermani and her team. They had all clearly benefited from their treatment with her. Beyond that, they all spontaneously talked about not only how helpful she was, but also how exceptionally caring she had been in comparison to other therapists they had known before.

Our collaboration continued for years. Dr. Martin Katzman, head of the START Clinic in Toronto where Monica was using Mindfulness Based Cognitive Behavior Therapy for severe anxiety disorders, encouraged us to further refine our breath-based intervention, now known as Breath-Body-Mind. By 2007 we began offering pro bono workshops with a not-for-profit, Serving Those Who Serve, to help relieve the physical and psychological problems that continued to plague those who were traumatized during and after the September 11, 2001, World Trade Center attacks—policemen, firemen, iron workers, Ground Zero workers, residents, and people who escaped from the towers. Years after the 2001 terrorist attacks, having failed to benefit from conventional treatments for post-traumatic stress disorder (PTSD), hundreds of people responded to the Breath-Body-Mind practices with significant improvements in their physical and psychological wellbeing. Dr. Vermani and Dr. Katzman generously volunteered their time to conduct two preliminary studies that documented these benefits. Since then, thousands more have benefited from these breath-centered mind-body practices.

We are very excited to see Dr. Vermani create a book that integrates her skills in Mindfulness Based Cognitive Behavior Therapy, her experience as a long-term serious yoga practitioner, her training as a Breath-Body-Mind teacher, and her naturally loving spirit. This well-organized, clearly written, and fully detailed book provides a very practical approach to giving people tools to relieve their suffering. Drawing from her extensive clinical experience and research, using both her mind and her heart, Dr. Vermani shows the way to a Deeper Wellness.

Follow this step-by-step approach to become the best you can be. Start with "How to use the book" and progress through the 18 chapters, which include lessons about your problems, goals, thoughts, emotions, obstacles, and valuing yourself. Useful exercises at the end of each chapter help you to personalize your understanding of how to create change in your life.

This book is the culmination of Dr. Vermani's professional experience and her loving nature. Here, therapists of diverse backgrounds will gather new ways to enrich their work. Those of you who may be struggling with anxiety or trauma will discover new perspectives and methods to build the skills needed to live happier lives. Some of you will do this on your own; others may engage with a therapist to work through the book. We will recommend this book to our patients and colleagues, confident that it can be a game changer for many of you.

Richard P. Brown, MD
Associate Professor of Clinical Psychiatry
Columbia University Vagelos College of Physicians and Surgeons, NY
& Patricia L. Gerbarg, MD
Assistant Professor of Clinical Psychiatry
New York Medical College, Valhalla, NY

Co-authors of *The Healing Power of the Breath, Non-Drug Treatments for ADHD*, and *Complementary and Integrative Treatments in Psychiatric Practices* (American Psychiatric Association Publishing)
www.Breath-Body-Mind.com

# INTRODUCTION

This book has been decades in the making.

The seeds of *A Deeper Wellness* took root over 25 years ago as I was working my way toward becoming a clinical psychologist. I was moved by an elderly gentleman who confided in me that he missed the good old days when his family doctor had the time to get to know him, knew the circumstances of his life in full, and asked how everything was going during appointments.

This man carried trauma from active duty on the battlefields of World War II and later struggled in his relationships. He confided to me that his current family doctor knew nothing about his life, that he felt rushed through short appointments, and that he was unable to remember half of what he had wanted to address in the doctor's office.

Moreover, he was never asked how things were going in his life. As a result, he was never allowed the opportunity to provide the context of his symptoms, which included stomach and digestive pain and dysfunction, muscle ache, and fatigue. Had he shared this information, his doctor might well have explored the possible — and highly likely — connection between his patient's physical symptoms and his undiagnosed anxiety and depressive disorder.

This sparked, for me, the question: Are primary-care physicians — through the time constraints of the existing system — missing the mind/body connection, and leaving serious mental health issues undiagnosed and untreated? What are the implications and costs both for patients and the medical system?

For my doctoral thesis, I conducted hundreds of interviews with patients in primary care waiting rooms, the first line of treatment for most people. The results were astounding. Over 50 percent of the patients interviewed were suffering from mental health issues undiagnosed by their primary care physician, including anxiety and major depressive disorders, bipolar and panic disorders.

We also weighed and measured patient medical records on file. These findings revealed that the heavier and thicker a patient's file, the more likely that patient wassuffering from an undiagnosed mental-health issue. Patients with undiagnosed mental health issues kept coming to their doctors to explore their physical symptoms, undergoing repeated tests, labs, check-ups, and evaluations, though the root causes of their symptoms were psychological, not physical.

The time constraints of brief primary care visits resulted in misdiagnoses. My doctoral thesis culminated in the creation of a short and simple diagnostic tool for general practitioners, to help them identify mental health patients, decrease suffering, and minimize the economic, medical, and societal costs to the healthcare system.

As I transitioned from academia into my clinical practice, I realized the need to help my patients understand the connection and interplay between their problems and their physical symptoms, persistent negative thoughts, and maladaptive behaviors.

I created the three-legged table schematic diagram, and took patients through the process of putting their problems on the table and identifying their symptoms represented by three legs: physical symptoms, negative thoughts, and harmful, maladaptive behaviors. To treat their problems, we began addressing all three 'legs' of the table.

This lesson evolved into the first chapter of this book, and the first step in helping people understand their symptoms, heal, and create the life they truly want. In full, the 18 chapters — or lessons — in *A Deeper Wellness* provide a way forward, a path to healing, that leads anyone ready and willing to do the work to a better, more authentic and joyful life.

Each of us has a life story. Regardless of the life you live — whether you are single, married, with or without children, over-working or unemployed — you have good moments and days and bad ones too. Positive and negative experiences are woven into the fabric of every life story.

In my 25 years as a clinical psychologist, I have had the unique privilege of working with hundreds of patients, helping them heal their past, deal with their present, and take control of their future.

Day by day, we are shaping the story of our lives. We let some people in, cast others aside. We open our hearts. We experience joy, sorrow, and loss. We expand. We contract. We soar. We fly high. And sometimes we crash and burn. Sometimes we pick ourselves up, dust ourselves off, learn from our experiences, set boundaries, and bring in resources and situations to help us be higher, better versions of ourselves. Other times, we remain stuck, repeating patterns until the suffering becomes unbearable and causes us to shift. These shifts reset our path, reconnect us to ourselves, and propel us along a wiser and more fruitful path.

We are all born alone and die alone. We take our first breath into the world alone, and our final breath out alone. Yes, we are born into a family, a culture, and a community. Once we are here our life expands out into the society into which we were born. We allow people into our journey. We shift and turn. We are born connected to our authentic selves and then, over time, our mind records and often personalizes events and our experiences with other people. We get caught up along our own path and growth in stories from experiences that distract us from our true self and purpose to grow. We often take on others' journeys as our own, which can create symptoms and suffering. Life has moments of pauses and flows, starts and stops, but the fabric of life is to simply propel you to grow and hopefully facilitate you to be your highest and best version of you.

The people around us are mirrors. They show us sides of ourselves we need to work on and reflect how far we have come in life and grown. Everything and everyone around us reflects, like a mirror, aspects of ourselves: our strengths, weaknesses, and opportunities for growth. The people we interact with reflect to us the attributes we need to acquire and the obstacles that hold us back from becoming the highest and best version of ourselves.

Suffering is a catalyst for change. As creatures of habit, we don't want to change, so the only way we propel and grow is through uncomfortable situations, challenges, and pain. A difficult work situation, unhealthy relationship dynamics, or illnesses … these are all lessons from which we learn and grow. But often we lose the lesson and cling to the pain and suffering that came along with it. And we live in fear of it repeating.

Our fears are simply self-doubts. Often, when we struggle, we doubt that we will have the ability to overcome life's challenges. We feel that holding onto our pain will prevent it from happening again, or at least make us better prepared for it. This is not true. We need to trust ourselves and know that we are built to survive and grow. Growth is more than size and age; we learn and grow from our life experiences and moments, each and every one of them, positive and negative.

The lessons in this book lead those who do the work into a deep sense of wellbeing, of confidence and connectedness to their authentic selves. We all have layers of traumas from which we can heal when we detach ourselves from our stories and connect to our opportunities for healing and growth. We are then free to manifest the life we deserve to live … and become the best version of ourselves.

Today I am a successful clinical psychologist, blessed with the opportunity to facilitate and witness many people's healings, struggles, and personal growth. As a psychologist, I help people to connect inward and work through their stories of pain, abandonment, loneliness, sadness, fear, anxiety, self-doubt, anger and feelings of inadequacies, and not feeling worthy of love … as we all are, just the way we are.

Therein lies the common ground I believe we share: we are all healing from negative stories, schemas, and 'recordings' we attach ourselves to in intense emotional moments, and intense affect and suffering. Life is a series of experiences, but we choose to label our experiences as positive or negative. The stories we create and negative cognitions we attach ourselves to are of our own creation. Since we create them, we can also rewrite and reframe them. And when we bring forth awareness, we can revise, shift, reframe, and heal them to be more positive, hopeful, and propelling cognitions and thoughts.

As you begin Chapter 1 of *A Deeper Wellness,* you are embarking on a journey of healing.

I wish you an insightful and rewarding journey through the many lessons of this book. As you work through the many tasks and challenges herein, I encourage you to stick with the process. You are worth it.

You are the reason I wrote this book. I cannot promise you that your journey through these lessons will be easy. But I do promise you that if you commit to the work at hand and your healing, you will acquire the skills and insights to reconnect with your authentic self, and find the courage and confidence to create the life you want.

Finally, I wish for you all that this book's title implies and holds: a deeper wellness.

With blessings,
Dr. Monica Vermani

# HOW TO USE THIS BOOK

We all lead busy lives. Day in and day out, caught up in the relentless pace of modern living, we can become so preoccupied with the demands of work, family, and finances that at times we feel overwhelmed. Mired in routines and habits and laden with responsibilities, we often lack the time and energy to take a breath, let alone think about the life we want.

The rapid, demanding pace of modern life can trigger states of stress, anxiety, worry, depression, restlessness, anger, and irritability ... and unhealthy habits, like overeating, overworking, avoidance, poor self-care, and addictions. Our daily responsibilities can leave us struggling to keep up with the demands of work, friends, and family, with little or no time for self-care or reflection. We find ourselves merely existing, not living the life we wish to live.

Most of us, when we are alone with our thoughts, worry about the future, construc worst-case scenarios, or ruminate on the past, replaying negative, self-deprecating thoughts over and over ... not exactly a recipe for being at peace or liking ourselves. True spirituality is an ability to connect with our authentic selves, be at peace with the content in our head, and enjoy our own company. Many of us, unfortunately, dislike spending time alone, when our minds ruminate on negative thoughts, disappointments, hurts and regrets, and feelings of not being good enough.

We all strive to live a life of balance and self-care. And we're drawn to the latest quick fixes and approaches that promise to help us take control, take better care, manage the stressors of modern life, implement better self-care, and bring wellness into our lives. But wellness is not a quick fix. Neither is it a placebo or a passing fancy. It's a serious undertaking. It's your very life!

*A Deeper Wellness* will help you stop just existing, and start living, and deal with the challenges you are facing now. The insights and self-reflective exercises at the end of each chapter will help you move beyond going through the motions in your life ... and begin to create meaningful change.

In each chapter, you will find a succinct explanation of the subject you will be exploring, along with accompanying exercises. You will learn how to identify your symptoms and how you can begin to take steps to break patterns of negative thinking and change the maladaptive, unhealthy behaviors and habits that no longer serve you and your highest self. Along the way, you may find yourself examining and challenging long-held negative thought patterns and beliefs. And you will learn to build life skills that allow you to break away from your negative thoughts and behaviors and begin to live the life you want.

Working through the exercises will help you think about your life through a new lens, facilitate the changes you would like to manifest, and embrace wellness and betterment across all areas of your life … work, school, family life, social life, intimacy, and self-care, which includes activities and pursuits that bring you joy, health, and spirituality.

While simple in nature, these exercises will ignite thought-provoking reflections and tasks that will challenge and engage you to think deeply and differently about your thoughts and behaviors, and imagine your best life, goals, and dreams by implementing change. So, sharpen your pencils, and allow yourself the time to do the work outlined in this book.

Allow yourself as much time as you need to complete each exercise before moving on to the next, and revisit the completed exercises whenever you like when further thoughts, memories, insights, or inspirations arise.

When we're in pain we spill onto others. It impacts every area of our lives. Taking charge and addressing your problems will positively affect every area of your life and everyone in it. Remember, *A Deeper Wellness* was created to help you bring forth meaningful change and happiness in your life. It's about you bringing true self-care and wellness to your life. May the attention and efforts you put into this work serve as your first steps in the direction of living a healthier, happier, more confident, successful, and balanced life. It's time to stop existing and start living!

Let's begin.

# A DEEPER WELLNESS

# CHAPTER 1
# PUTTING YOUR
# PROBLEMS ON THE TABLE

The first step to forging a deeper wellness and creating positive change in your life is building awareness. To do this, let's begin by putting your problems on the table. Recognizing the problems and challenges that prevent you from living a full and happy life is the first step in creating positive change. In this chapter, we'll explore the relationship between your problems and your symptoms. As you work through the exercise at the end of the chapter, you can begin to set goals that will allow you to make the changes you desire for your healing, recovery, and betterment.

We walk through life with many symptoms, often feeling overwhelmed. As we undertake to do the work of creating positive change, it's important to take stock, look deeply at ourselves, and identify our problems and corresponding symptoms. Looking at symptoms can seem overwhelming, but it is necessary. After all, the first step to betterment is awareness. The goal of this book is to help you shift towards betterment.

Let's simplify this process.

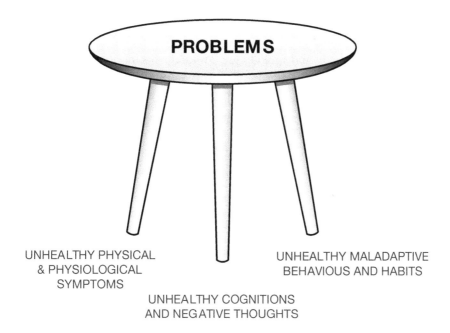

**WHY THREE LEGS**

Here is a table with three legs. You're going to put your problems on the tabletop, any-thing and everything … whatever is troubling you, from work struggles, low self-esteem, relationship troubles, interpersonal conflicts, anger, medical conditions, addictions (e.g., food, alcohol, porn, shopping, video games, etc.), chronic pain, money concerns, depres-sion, anxiety, infertility. Dive deep into yourself. Be honest and commit to this task.

Give yourself as much time as you need to identify what is truly troubling you. We may, at times, get in the way of our healing. Step out of the way for your betterment; be honest and transparent with yourself.

I use the image of a three-legged table because problems manifest in our lives in three distinct ways: physical and physiological symptoms in our bodies; negative thoughts and cognitions in our minds; and unhealthy, maladaptive behaviors, actions, and lifestyle habits.

Should you decide to address your physical symptoms while ignoring your negative thoughts and behaviors, you continue to support the negative thoughts and behaviors at play in your life. Dynamics don't shift, and we don't facilitate significant changes. Like-wise, if you choose to change your behaviors while ignoring your physical and cognitive symptoms, you unwittingly and unwillingly continue to support your problems. If you treat just one of the 'legs' on its own and ignore the others, you continue to prop up the negative forces at play. But when you confront all three categories of the three-legged table, you empower yourself to make the significant changes you want in your life to be who you want to be.

We can treat, revise, and reframe our negative thoughts with Cognitive Therapy (CT), thereby breaking that table leg, or alter our maladaptive behaviors with Behavioral Therapy (BT), and break that one. Either way, the table can remain standing, and we can remain stuck.

The far more effective option — Cognitive Behavioral Therapy (CBT) — is a form of therapy that breaks both legs, and in doing so shifts the recipient of treatment towards real, meaningful, positive changes. CBT works by challenging and reframing the thoughts you hold onto, and, in addition, promoting you to start facilitating positive changes by slowly shifting our maladaptive behaviors and habits to healthier, more adaptive ones.

With this knowledge, let's get to work, and put your problems on the table. Don't focus on just a few problems. Be transparent and honest with yourself. List all of your problems, regardless of their magnitude or severity.

## LEG #1: PHYSICAL AND PHYSIOLOGICAL SYMPTOMS

Physical and physiological symptoms — represented by the first leg of the table — encompass the symptoms that occur in the body. These include headaches, muscle aches, weakness, tingling, numbness and tensions, abdominal distress (including diarrhea, constipation or cramping, and nausea) fatigue, heart palpitations, shortness of breath, restlessness, anxiety, concentration or memory problems, racing mind, sexual dysfunction, fatigue, moodiness, crying, sadness, irritability, and panic attacks. Panic attacks are severe forms of incidents and situations where you feel a number of physical symptoms coming on, peaking, and dropping in intensity. People often feel as though they're having a heart attack when, in fact, they are experiencing a panic (or anxiety) attack. Once you've had a panic attack, you constantly worry about having another one as they feel like they come out of the blue.

## LEG #2: COGNITIVE SYMPTOMS, NEGATIVE THOUGHTS

The middle leg represents our cognitive thoughts, more specifically, negative, unhealthy ones. We are born into a household and a unique family environment. In this unique environment as we grow, we learn our values and thoughts about the world. We observe the way our parents demonstrate love, deal with conflicts, and cope with life's challenges.

For example, if Mom was a clean freak, we absorb that value, or if Dad drank at the end of a hard day, we take on the thought that this is how to cope with stress. In the unique setting of the home environment, we not only learn our values, habits, and behaviors, we develop our thoughts and beliefs.

Then, as we move through our own life experiences, when we encounter hurts, sufferings, and failures, such as job loss, heartaches, significant injuries, bullying, grief, loss, and disappointments, we internalize and personalize these experiences, and often develop negative thoughts which lead to self-depreciation, feelings of hopelessness or worthlessness, and negative thoughts about our abilities, relationships, the world, and opportunities.

Persistent negative thoughts like:

- *Men are*
- *Women are*
- *Children are*
- *My family is*
- *Relationships are*
- *I'm not good enough*
- *I'm ugly*
- *I'm a failure*
- *I will never amount to anything*
- *I am not worthy of love*
- *I'm stupid*
- *I'm incapable*
- *I'm unlucky*
- *I cannot change*
- *Everybody else has it better than me*
- *I'm a fraud, an impostor*

A very common negative thought is, 'I am undeserving of …' money, happiness, a relationship, success. These negative thoughts are what we're looking at here. Dig deep. Think about your negative thoughts. How are you self-depreciative?

## LEG #3: MALADAPTIVE BEHAVIORS

So far, we've talked about physical symptoms and the negative thoughts racing in our heads. Finally, we are going to examine how this plays out on a day-to-day basis through unhealthy, maladaptive behaviors and habits.

Maladaptive behaviors include:

- eating too much
- eating too little
- sleeping too much or too little
- relying on alcohol and drugs to numb physical symptoms or escape negative thoughts
- avoiding relationships or staying in a negative relationship
- not communicating our needs
- angry outbursts
- avoiding confrontation
- self-sabotage
- people pleasing
- not setting boundaries
- staying in a job we don't like
- avoiding career advancement
- poor self-care
- procrastination
- neglecting health
- self-harm
- insensitive and impulsive behaviors
- cheating on a partner
- dropping out of school
- poor financial management
- poor decision-making
- inflicting or tolerating abuse
- poor hygiene
- not getting the medical treatment one needs

And the list goes on…

I know that these lists are overwhelming … and that we walk around with these symptoms affecting us day after day. But the good news is that by identifying our symptoms in these three categories we can begin to address them. We can use the three-legged table to gain insight into and awareness of the connections between our problems and our physical symptoms, negative thoughts, and maladaptive behaviors. It's time to put your problems on the table and address them. Let's get to it.

**In the exercise at the end of this chapter, you will explore your physical symptoms, negative thoughts, and maladaptive behaviors.**

## THE GOOD NEWS

Here's the good news: when you've identified your physical symptoms, negative thoughts, and unhealthy behaviors, you can then begin to address specific symptoms in a manageable way. From there, you can begin to set goals. (A goal is simply where you would like to be in your life.) You can then begin to take small, achievable actions, steps forward from where you are to where you want to be. In the exercise at the end of this chapter, we will focus on creating goals and the steps you can take to create incremental, positive changes.

## SUPPORTING CHANGE

Let's look at some of the therapies and actions you can take that will support change for your betterment.

## PHYSICAL

First, if you're experiencing physical symptoms, healthy symptom-management possibilities include medication, exercise, and other self-care routines and meditation practices.

Depending on your symptoms, you could find medications that will alleviate the intensity of your troublesome physical symptoms. Medication throws a blanket over your symptoms to lessen their intensity, and it also has a reparative function when used in combination with therapeutic treatments. Medication alone breaks one leg of our table. Alone, it is never enough to effect significant change.

Meditation allows us to sit with uncomfortable sensations rather than avoiding or distracting ourselves from them. In meditation, we focus on our breath and remaining in the present moment. Your breath is the only thing that takes place from moment to moment. Physical exercise, such as yoga, walking, cardio, weight training, and even simple breathing exercises, just like meditation, enables us to focus on the present moment and offers physical benefits, replenishment, calmness, and renewal.

## COGNITIVE DISTORTIONS

Let's look at what we can do about our cognitive distortions, better known as persistent negative thoughts. We all struggle with negative thoughts, that is to say persistent, harmful ways of seeing ourselves and our prospects. Remember, we all grow up in unique families and live through life events that can negatively shape our worldview, self-image, and self-esteem. Identifying these negative thoughts is the first step towards creating positive change in our lives.

Negative automatic thoughts, such as: *I'm not good enough, I'm not capable, I can't handle this, I'm a failure, I am weak,* or *I'm not smart enough,* over time can wreak havoc in our lives. Remember, what we focus on expands and begins to feel true. Twisted thinking and overgeneralizations, such as: *Everybody else has it easier than me;* sweeping negative generalizations about our prospects, such as: *Nothing ever goes my way, I never make a good first impression,* or *I'll never attract a good partner;* and cognitive distortions, such as: *I'm a total mess, I never get the recognition I deserve, Life's just too hard, People always leave me for someone better, smarter, or better looking,* hold us back from taking the chances and making the connections that can lead to success, fulfillment, and happiness. When we are children, our innocence leads us to strive and believe we can have it all. We acquire negativity through modeled behaviors, hardships, or personalizing life's challenges.

## IT IS NOT WRITTEN IN STONE

Your negative thoughts are not written in stone. The automatic negative thoughts, twisted thinking, and cognitive distortions that cycle through your head are of your own creation. You choose to hold onto them and reinforce them. But you have power over them, and you can replace them with more positive thoughts that better serve you. What you put out there, you will manifest. Think about your pervasive, limiting negative thoughts. Identify those that trouble you and hold you back, thoughts that you would like to change. Make sure that what you're putting out into the world is what you want to manifest, not what you fear or dread.

As an experiment, think of times you feel good about yourself. That feeling is like a pebble you throw in the water; the ripple effect makes people gravitate towards you. On an off day, the opposite happens.

While we often feel overwhelmed by our negative thoughts, behaviors, and physical symptoms, there are plenty of things that we can do to help support the change we wish to manifest in our lives. There are things we're all aware of, such as starting or increasing an exercise regimen, confiding in a supportive friend, colleague, or family member, sleeping and eating well, socializing and seeking mutual support through a buddy system, making healthier choices, introducing self-care into your life, seeking out ways to get involved in your community, or seeking medical or psychological counseling. All are worth exploring.

I would like to share with you a few words about creating change. We don't live in isolation, and any change we begin to make is going to impact other people in our lives, like the ripple effect when you throw a pebble into the water. From some aspects of your life, you will find help, including friends, a supportive employer, access to resources, perhaps the fortuitous timing of events — such as a gym opening in your neighborhood just as you resolve to finally commit to an exercise routine — and your own degree of motivation.

Likewise, among friends, family members, and colleagues, we are likely to find saboteurs, including non-supportive individuals who are threatened by change, overwhelming and conflicting work, family, and social obligations, lack of available resources, discouragement after small set-backs, self-sabotaging settings, situations, and individuals, and lack of peer support. Take charge of the energy in your space and surroundings. Stay close to supportive people who are aligned with your positivity and goals of betterment.

**In the exercise at the end of this chapter, you'll be asked to list some of the obstacles you anticipate.**

It's important to take a good look at the people in your life, and the environments where you work, live, and play. Where do you anticipate running into difficulties while making the changes you want to make? Who and where in your life will you find support as you move toward your goal? Explore!

Take the time to work through the exercise at the end of this chapter. As you move into creating change in your life, remember that change is a process with challenges and rewards. Allow yourself time, patience, and compassion to work toward your goal. Reinforcement strengthens our determination and commitment. Revisit this chapter from time to time and review the challenges and goals that you identified and set for yourself in the course of completing this exercise. Ask yourself how much closer to your goal are you today than when you began. What are the next steps that will take you closer to your goal? Revisit this chapter to reinforce your commitment to change, reset your goals and strategies, and put any new problems you are facing on the table.

I regularly have mini meetings with me, a date with myself, for my betterment, over tea on my balcony. I explore where I am, the obstacles to my growth, and what new steps I want to take toward my goals of betterment.

Nobody can go back and start over from the beginning, but you can start today to make a new ending. By changing nothing, nothing changes. A year from now, you'll be glad you started today. Let's start!

## EXERCISE

What are the main problems in your life? Take your time to honestly explore the areas in your life where you are suffering or struggling.

Think about the problems that are currently troubling you. List them. Dive deep into yourself. Be honest and commit to this task. Identify what is truly troubling you. Take as much time as you need.

_____

_____

_____

_____

_____

_____

_____

_____

Are you experiencing troubling psychological/physical symptoms? If so, list them.

_____

_____

_____

_____

_____

_____

_____

_____

Think about your negative thoughts. List them.

_____

_____

_____

_____

_____

_____

_____

_____

Think about your unhealthy habits or troubling behaviors. List them.

_____

_____

_____

_____

_____

_____

_____

_____

Once you have identified your problems, symptoms, negative thoughts, and maladaptive habits and behaviors, you will start to recognize the interrelationships at play.

Further, you can begin challenging your negative thoughts and change the harmful patterns and behaviors at play in your life. Your symptoms can feel overwhelming, but by sorting them into categories, you can see them and set incremental goals to treat each one.

You don't need to cure yourself, just focus on taking baby steps toward change to help move you in the right direction: health, healing, and betterment for your overall quality of life.

# CHAPTER 2
# YOUR IDEAL SELF

In Chapter 1, we explored our problems, which led to physical symptoms, and examined how our negative thoughts and maladaptive behaviors manifest in our lives. We have begun a process of changing our lives for the better. In this chapter, we explore the ideal you. Everything is a process, and we are beginning to understand that by dealing with our symptoms, we can learn to make better decisions and live a healthier life.

We live in a fast-paced, demanding world and we are expected to hang in there, stay strong, and carry on. We sometimes get stuck in patterns and deal with our symptoms as best we can, day in and day out. But how do we know when our symptoms are a big deal?

Here's the answer to this daunting question: our symptoms are a big deal when they cause suffering, impede functioning on a day-to-day basis, and prevent us from living a fuller and better quality of life.

Anything that hinders your daily life, and negatively impacts your life tasks, such as work, interpersonal relationships, and your spirituality is a big deal. If you're experiencing irritability, sleeplessness, anxiety, depression, or dealing with an addiction to shopping, food, alcohol, or drugs, your symptoms are a big deal. But nothing is static. We're always shifting and changing, so let's shift with health in mind.

We all have life tasks, including work, school, family life, social life, intimacy, self-care, and spirituality (by which I mean connecting with our spirit, or our 'self,' liking our own company, being at peace with our own mind). At times we can become stuck in maladaptive thoughts or behaviors, and find ourselves at a loss as to how to find our way out.

## WAVING THE MAGIC WAND

When getting to know clients in my private practice, I ask them to imagine that I could wave a magic wand and take away all of their problems. Then, I ask them to imagine life with their problems magically obliterated. We explore where they are and where they want to be. In the gap lie their problematic symptoms (physical symptoms, negative thoughts, and maladaptive, unhealthy behaviors). How would they describe where they'd want to go in life? Who would they like to be? What would they like to be doing?

**In the exercise at the end of this chapter, you'll be tapping into your deepest desires and imagining the ideal you.**

What may on the surface appear to be a fanciful exercise is a valuable, life-changing assignment. Defining where you want to go is essentially goal setting … and setting goals plants the seeds for positive, meaningful changes. If I could wave a magic wand and take away all of your problems, what would your life look like?

I am going to ask you to dream big and describe your ideal life in many areas. Where would you like to be? What would it look like? How would you feel? Take your time with this. Write it all down and enjoy the process! Here are your categories: work/school, social, family, intimacy, self-care, hobbies and interests, health (physical and mental), spirituality, money, confidence, and boundaries.

Defining where you want to go in life shines a spotlight on the gap between where you are and where you want to be, and gives you a start and an endpoint to help you set a course to close that gap.

**The next exercise will help illuminate how your symptoms could be holding you back from getting where you want to go.**

You will be taking stock of where you are now and noting the gap between your current reality and your ideal self. Be as honest as you can with yourself. The more realistically you capture your current circumstances, the better you will be able to identify the gaps between where you are and where you want to be in various aspects of your life. As we move into the next step, you'll find there's gold in your gaps.

Next, compare your ideal with your current life, and choose one area of your life in which you would like to start to affect healthy, positive change today, and move closer toward your ideal. Choose one area of your life in which you wish to commit to implementing healthy change.

## HARD BUT NOT IMPOSSIBLE

Change is hard — but it is not impossible. The good news here is that you know four important things that you didn't know before you began this lesson: where you are, where you want to be, the symptoms you need to alleviate, and the changes you have to make in your life to take you where you want to go.

To make the changes you are committed to making, you may find that you need help. If you'd like to improve your health and physical fitness, you may want to join a gym, a running group, or sign up for a yoga class. Before doing any of that, you may wish to visit your family doctor or consult a nutritionist. If you're looking to improve your finances, you may wish to talk to a financial adviser or your bank manager. If you'd like to work on improving relationships within your family, you may want to seek one-on-one or family counseling. Or, if you're looking to build self-confidence to advance your career, you may look for a professional advisor who can assist you in building the image, social skills, and confidence you require. You need to focus on things in order to better them because they won't shift and resolve on their own. We do the best with what we have and what we know. Learning from others helps us know more. Make a list of the people, resources, and professional supports that can help you begin to make changes in the areas of your life you are ready to work on.

When it comes to creating change in our lives, two major factors come into play: your faith in yourself and your ability to make a change, and your fear of the unknown, of possible failure, of obstacles you think you have, or lack of confidence in your ability to commit to change or to succeed. Here's a motivational thought to help sustain you as you work toward your goal: *Make your faith bigger than your fear*. Faith is belief in yourself and your skillset, and fear is self-doubt.

As you move into creating change in your life, keep in mind that change is a process that is both challenging and rewarding. Allow yourself time and patience to work toward your ideal life. Remember, as you move away from the thoughts and behaviors that no longer serve you, you may be afraid of what lies ahead … but that's okay. Your faith in yourself will carry you through the tough moments. Remember: Make your faith bigger than your fear. Most of us have self-esteem struggles, but we can learn to parent and nurture ourselves. We can treat ourself with compassion and love, and take steps toward the life we deserve. Return to this chapter — and your notes — from time to time. Revisit the goals and strategies that you laid out for yourself here today. See how much closer to your goal you are today than when you began. Use these resources to connect to and reinforce your commitment to change, and to reset your goals and strategies.

## EXERCISE

If you could wave a magic wand and take away all of your problems, what would your life look like? Describe your ideal life in the following areas. Where would you like to be? What would it look like? How would you feel? The future is imagination. Imagine manifesting the best version of your life … the life you dream of for yourself. Don't think of obstacles or whether or not it is possible. What would your ideal life be like if you could manifest it now?

## WORK/CAREER/SCHOOL:

SOCIAL/FAMILY:

INTIMACY:

_____
_____
_____
_____
_____
_____
_____
_____
_____
_____
_____

SELF-CARE/INTERESTS:

_____
_____
_____
_____
_____
_____
_____
_____
_____
_____
_____
_____

SPIRITUALITY/ENJOYING MY OWN COMPANY:

_____
_____
_____
_____
_____
_____
_____
_____

MONEY:

_____
_____
_____
_____
_____
_____
_____
_____
_____

CONFIDENCE:

_____
_____
_____
_____
_____
_____
_____
_____
_____
_____

BOUNDARIES:

_____
_____
_____
_____
_____
_____
_____
_____
_____
_____
_____

Describe your current life in the same areas.

Defining where you want to go in life illuminates the gap between where you are and where you want to be, and provides both the start and the endpoint to help you set a course to close that gap. (This exercise helps illuminate the factors that could be holding you back from getting where you want to go.)

## WORK/CAREER/SCHOOL:

SOCIAL/FAMILY:

_____

_____

_____

_____

_____

_____

_____

_____

_____

INTIMACY:

_____

_____

_____

_____

_____

_____

_____

_____

_____

SELF-CARE/INTERESTS:

_____

_____

_____

_____

_____

_____

_____

_____

_____

SPIRITUALITY/ENJOYING MY OWN COMPANY:

_____

_____

_____

_____

_____

_____

_____

_____

_____

MONEY:

_____

_____

_____

_____

_____

_____

_____

_____

_____

_____

CONFIDENCE:

_____

_____

_____

_____

_____

_____

_____

_____

_____

_____

_____

## BOUNDARIES:

_____

_____

_____

_____

_____

_____

_____

_____

_____

Now, you can begin to set a course to close the gap between your current self and where you ideally want to be. Make a list of changes that you can start to make — right now — to move toward becoming your 'ideal' self. Don't let yourself become overwhelmed; take baby steps.

# CHAPTER 3
# UNDERSTANDING STRESS & INTEGRATING SELF-CARE

Stress: it's something we all have, and something we all struggle with in some capacity. It's an unavoidable part of life. And we could all benefit from strategies to cope with it. In this chapter, we're going to examine our stress. We'll talk about exactly what stress is and learn life-changing strategies to help deal with it.

Stress is the result of our activity level surpassing our energy level. When this happens, we have two options: we can decrease our activity level — mental or physical activity, and the responsibilities we take on — or we can increase our energy. Option one — decreasing our activity level — is often not an option. After all, life comes with responsibilities and activities we need to fulfill for survival. We have to go to work, and we have things we need to do to sustain life for ourselves and our families. Option two — raising our energy level — makes more sense, and we can take charge of this area.

There are four sources of energy: food/nourishment, sleep/rest, exercise and breathing, and actively maintaining a calm state of mind (addressing our problems rather than avoiding them). Often, we don't realize how depleted we are feeling, and how much all we take on and carry drains our energy. Take a moment to think about situations in your life that stress you out. What springs to mind?

## COPING WITH STRESS

Once you've identified your sources of stress, you'll quickly surmise that while you may be able to eliminate some stressors, most of your responsibilities are not going to go away any time soon. The way to cope with stressors in life is to increase our energy. How do we do that? Let's look closer at our energy sources.

## NOURISHMENT AND THE FOOD WE EAT

Number one is the food we eat. We often eat food to fill our bellies, but we don't necessarily choose quality foods that provide energy and nourishment. Instead, we reach for overly processed foods that spike our insulin levels, or stimulants, such as caffeine-laden coffee or chocolate or other sugary treats that give us a little boost. We often choose carb-heavy comfort foods that make us sluggish over nutrient-rich foods that give us the energy we need to get through a stressful day.

When making choices, it is important to consider the foods we eat as a source of energy. Ask yourself:

- *Am I eating foods that will give me the energy level I need?*
- *Will what I am about to eat sustain my energy level throughout the day?*
- *Am I eating food just to fill my belly?*
- *Do I rely on caffeine and sugar to keep me running when I'm sluggish or sleepy?*

**SLEEP/REST**

Speaking of sleep, it's our second source of energy. Often, without realizing it, we deprive ourselves of quality sleep. When it comes to raising our energy levels, sleep is a big deal. Why? Because sleep gives us rejuvenation. Quality sleep is crucial in helping to raise our energy levels to sustain our day-to-day activities. It's when we rejuvenate, replenish, and repair our bodies after the wear and tear of the day. When we sleep, we move through cycles of light and deep sleep. In deep sleep, called REM (rapid eye movement), we repair our central nervous system and muscles. And when we're sick, sleep helps rebuild and recharge our immune systems. That's why we need to sleep more than usual when we have a cold or the flu or other infections, or when we need to heal.

Through poor sleep hygiene, we deprive ourselves of much-needed sleep. Eating just before bed, for example, stimulates the metabolism which, in turn, keeps us awake. Exercising before bed also raises our energy levels and gets in the way of sleep. And these days a growing source of poor sleep hygiene is technology. Though it may feel relaxing, binge-watching movies or TV shows on our laptops or phones, or scrolling through Facebook and other social media just before closing our eyes stimulates our minds and can keep us awake into the wee hours rather than helping us wind down and fall asleep peacefully.

We go, go, go throughout the day. Then, overworked, overstressed, and overstimulated by our electronic devices, we jump into bed hoping to sleep. How does that work? We need to realize that, especially when our day has been super active, we need to define a period of time before we go to bed where we wind down and arrive at a place of calmness, ready for rest, relaxation, and deep, quality sleep.

Winding down before bed allows you to empty your mind, calm down, and relax your body. Turn off the lights and prepare for quality sleep. No TV, reading, or catching up on social media. Your bedroom is really for two things: intimate recreational activities and sleep.

You should not be reading books. You should not be watching TV. You should not be on your phone. You should not be worrying about the next day. In bed, if you don't have intimacy going on, you should be asleep. If you are not asleep within 5 or 10 minutes of going to bed, you should get out of bed and go to another room. Allow yourself to become drowsy, then go back to bed. Look at your quality of rest as a means to calm your mind and recharge your body's energy level for the day ahead. Many people say that in bed, their minds race with worries. A useful exercise before bedtime is to grab a notepad and create a worry log. Just dump from your head onto the paper all your worries. Place it aside and say you will address these matters in the morning, then plant an intention to allow yourself to rest and renew with a clear mind to be awake and refreshed to face a new day.

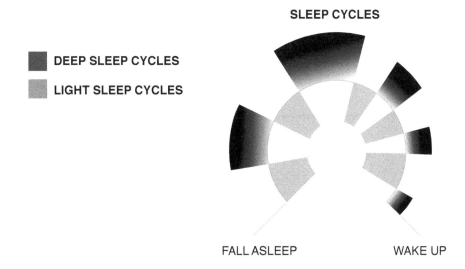

**SLEEP CYCLES**

■ **DEEP SLEEP CYCLES**

■ **LIGHT SLEEP CYCLES**

FALL ASLEEP　　　　WAKE UP

## BREATH

Our third source of energy is exercise and breathing. One reason we feel so great after a workout is because exercise forces us to take full, deep body breaths. Throughout the day, especially when we're under stress, we're running around, taking short and shallow breaths, no deeper than chest level. This is an unhealthy breathing pattern as the resulting lack of oxygen to the muscles prevents us from feeling our best.

When we breathe deeply, bringing our breath down to our belly, we are relaxing and rejuvenating. When we do cardio, Pilates, or yoga, or go for a brisk walk or run, we are forcing our bodies to counter the stress response of short and shallow breaths. We're literally going deeper, breathing more deeply. These deep breaths restore and rejuvenate every muscle in the body and calm the mind. But we don't need exercise to breathe a little deeper. Thoughtfully, from time to time throughout your day, take a moment and pay attention to your breath. Breathe deeply. You will feel your stress level lower immediately.

## STATE OF MIND

This brings us to the fourth and final source of energy: a calm state of mind. But how do we get there? Doesn't just hearing someone tell you to calm down stress you out? One of the goals of *A Deeper Wellness* is to help you clean up your life and foster a calm state of mind by addressing issues, dealing with past hurts or disappointments, and looking at life in new ways to help deal with situations, feelings, and challenges that are problematic in your life. *Am I paying my taxes on time? Am I dealing with relationship struggles? Am I doing okay at work? Am I taking care of myself?*

Just as exercise and breathing calm the mind, so too does meditation. Spending some time with yourself engaging in an activity can lead you to a calm state of mind. When you spend time with yourself, alone with your thoughts, what comes up? Are you worried about things? Are you stressed out? Do you ruminate, imagining worst-case scenarios? Or are you feeling at peace? Can you plant a seed of hope for good in your own life and the world? It's important to prioritize yourself and begin to introduce self-care that allows you to feel calm and at peace in your daily life.

## A FEW WORDS ABOUT GUILT

A few words about something that can be a major source of stress in our lives: guilt. Out of guilt, we often put others ahead of ourselves. Next time you're feeling guilty, take a minute to examine your guilt. Ask yourself: *What do I want, as opposed to what other people want of me? Am I putting someone else's needs before my own?* When we choose to do so, it's okay. But when you don't want to and push yourself to make others happy at your expense, it becomes a problem you need to address. It's poor self-care and self-love.

Putting other people ahead of yourself is not good self-care. We are born alone, and we die alone. We're also born into a world, and into a family. But your journey is your own, a self-revolution; it's about you learning how to be your highest and best self. Everyone is learning and sometimes we handicap others' growth by giving in to guilt. Then you become a part of their problem of lack of growth.

Guilt is a signal that there's a conflict between what you want for yourself and what others want from you. The goal is to put yourself first. Ask yourself: *Am I prioritizing my needs and goals? Are there situations or people in my life that often leave me feeling guilty?*

## AN ENERGY AUDIT

Explore the four sources of energy in your life and where you are — and are not — prioritizing yourself and practicing good self-care. This information will give you a snapshot of your current energy-enhancing habits and routines — aspects of your life that impact your sources of energy — right now.

**In the exercise at the end of this chapter, you will explore your sources of energy, and the changes you can make to improve your energy levels and support your best life.**

Are your food habits good, fair, or problematic? Do they need some attention? Do alcohol, drugs, or other substance habits negatively impact your energy level and/or quality of life?

Examine the quality of your sleep. Are you getting enough sleep? Are you prioritizing it? Do you struggle with serious insomnia or other sleep issues that should be addressed? A family doctor can arrange a sleep study to determine if there is a problem that can be addressed medically.

Look at your exercise regimens and breathing habits. Are you getting some exercise every day? Are you paying attention to your breath, or rushing around throughout the day stressed, taking short, shallow breaths?

What is your state of mind? Are you addressing things from the past that bother you? Are you forgiving people; are you forgiving yourself? Do you have compassion for how heavy your life can sometimes feel?

Take a look at the role of guilt in your life. Are you prioritizing what you want for yourself over what others want from you? Are you able to refuse a request from someone who wants something from you that you do not want to give?

Do you often give in to the demands of others to your detriment? Many of us become co-dependent when we derive our value from taking care of others or take on roles as people-pleasers to be liked by others. Explore your patterns.

## MORE ABOUT GUILT

I'd like to share a few more insights about guilt. Remember, when it comes to guilt, ask yourself whether you are putting the needs of others ahead of your own. If you are, it's not only detrimental to you, it's also detrimental to the person you're giving in to. Here's why: every time you put the needs of another person ahead of yourself you prevent that person from learning lessons. Give in to guilt, and you not only put yourself on the back burner, which is just poor self-care, you also negatively impact the other person in the situation. No one wins.

Here's an example: I want to wear a black shirt to the family Holiday party. I put on the black shirt — no problem. But then my mother comes around and says, "Hey, I bought you this beautiful white shirt, and I'd like you to wear it tonight." I decline and tell her I prefer what I've chosen. She responds: "Please … for me?" Is it such a big deal to make your mother happy?" Suddenly, out of the blue, there's conflict. Guilt shows up. If I cave in and wear the white shirt, I sacrifice what I want for myself. But if I follow what I want, I feel petty, and disappoint my mother by doing what I want rather than what she wants of me.

It might not be a big deal to change my shirt. But my mother needs to realize that I am a grown adult, and I should be allowed to make my own choices. Every time I give in to even the smallest request, I prevent her from realizing that her child is an adult and entitled to her own opinion: she doesn't get the opportunity to let go a little and see me as an adult rather than a child. On my end, every time I sacrifice myself, I disappoint myself. This leads to feelings of unhappiness, sadness, discontent, and anger toward somebody else for wanting something different for me than I want for myself.

## EXAMINING GUILT

Think about a situation in your life where you feel guilty, perhaps a recurring situation with a specific person, something that troubles you, something you would like to change. When you give in to what the other person in this situation wants, what is this person failing to learn? How do you feel? Now, imagine standing up for what you want in this guilt-inducing scenario. Consider standing your ground the next time this situation presents itself and loving yourself enough to live your life for yourself.

At the end of this chapter, you'll have an opportunity to examine a recurring source of guilt in your life and develop a strategy to deal with it for your own benefit, and for the benefit of the person who wants something of you that you do not wish to give.

## CONSIDER MEDITATION

There's a very powerful way to gain control and calm our minds when we're feeling stressed, overwhelmed, or exhausted: meditate. You may already be familiar with the practice of meditation, but I want you to be aware that you can use various meditation practices throughout your day. Different types of meditation allow you to connect to the present moment completely. If you're new to meditation, explore the various types of meditation out there, and pick the style or styles that align with your character, personality, and lifestyle.

We've covered a lot of ground here. You have lots to think about and do to create self-care routines that raise your energy levels and reduce stress in your life. Before we conclude, take a minute to review and reflect on the new insights you have gained. Remember, as you begin to create change in your life, change is a process with both challenges and rewards. Allow yourself time, patience, and compassion to work toward your goals.

Revisit this chapter and your notes from time to time. Review the insights and strategies you've discovered. These notes can help you reinforce your commitment to yourself, work through any obstacles you are facing, and create new goals and strategies. Finally, remember that nobody can go back and start over at the beginning, but you can start today and make a new ending. Start where you're at. Let's do this!

## EXERCISE

With a snapshot of the strengths and weaknesses in your day-to-day self-care, you can begin to look at ways to raise your energy levels to help you deal with your stress. Set goals. These goals will guide you to take steps forward and begin to shift from where you are to where you want to be. The focus here is on incremental, positive change.

### ENERGY:

There are four sources of energy: food, sleep, exercise and breathing, and state of mind. List areas where you could make improvements to build your energy levels:

### FOOD/NOURISHMENT:

_____

_____

_____

_____

_____

_____

_____

_____

_____

_____

SLEEP/REST:

_____
_____
_____
_____
_____
_____
_____
_____
_____
_____
_____

EXERCISE AND BREATHING:

_____
_____
_____
_____
_____
_____
_____
_____
_____

## A CALM STATE OF MIND:

_____

_____

_____

_____

_____

_____

_____

_____

Examine your guilt. Think of a recurring scenario in your life that causes you guilt. Examine the dynamics of this situation. Think about the gap between what you want and what someone else wants of you. Think of how you could handle this situation differently the next time it shows up in your life.

_____

_____

_____

_____

_____

_____

_____

Set goals to raise your energy levels and introduce better self-care into your daily life.

_____

_____

_____

_____

_____

_____

_____

_____

_____

_____

_____

_____

_____

_____

_____

_____

_____

_____

_____

_____

# CHAPTER 4
# IT'S THE THOUGHT THAT COUNTS

Our thoughts are powerful. One thought at a time, our thoughts — both positive and negative — shape our lives. Positive thinking propels us forward, while negative thinking feeds our fears and self-doubts, and holds us back from attaining personal growth, happiness, and success. Conquering fear and self-doubt are all about replacing negative thoughts with positive ones.

In this chapter, we're going to examine our negative thoughts. We need to understand that life is a series of experiences. We tend to judge or label our experiences as positive or negative. The reason we judge an experience as negative is that we perceive it as something that has somehow inconvenienced us.

The same experience could be judged as positive or negative depending on your circumstances and state of mind. Here's an example: my kid comes to me and says: "Mommy, Mommy, I heard the boogieman walking around upstairs. Please come upstairs so I can change into my pjs." If my day is running smoothly, and we're having a good time, and I'm rested and not pressed for time, I might say: "Sure, let's go chase him off." The situation is positive. My kid's kind of cute, and I'm happy to go upstairs and chase down the boogieman.

But if I'm under the gun, if I also have to cook dinner, clean the house, and supervise my kid's homework, the boogieman situation is not cute at all. It just makes me irritated and frustrated. It is inconvenient for me to stop making dinner and go upstairs to look for the boogieman. This time, I label the boogieman experience as negative, not just a lighthearted thing to deal with.

Remember, life is a series of experiences that, depending on our circumstances and state of mind, we label as positive or negative. Often we fail to realize that our negative experiences — meaning those that we judge as negative — are the ones that help us change. That's right — our negative experiences act as a catalyst for change, to help us be a better, higher version of ourselves, or help us learn a new skillset that is beneficial for our lives.

## THOUGHTS AND PERCEPTIONS

Throughout our lives, we constantly accumulate thoughts and perceptions. Some are the result of our upbringing, some from our life experiences, others from societal influences, such as our culture, the economy, our parents, our grandparents, our peer groups, mass media, and social media. Nothing is static. As we age, we develop new skills, have new experiences, enter new phases in life, and we shift our states and perceptions.

We need to start to examine and challenge our thoughts rather than digest every entrenched thought as if it were an indisputable truth written in stone. Here's a visual representation to help us understand where thoughts come from and help us look at and challenge our ingrained thoughts.

**In the exercise at the end of this chapter, you'll explore your automatic thoughts, core beliefs, and other negative thoughts at play in your life.**

LEAVES: POSITIVE & NEGATIVE
AUTOMATIC THOUGHTS

BRANCHES:
THE VARIOUS ROLES
WE PLAY/TAKE ON IN LIFE

ROOTS: CORE BELIEFS WE
DEVELOP FROM OUR YOUTH

We are our thoughts. Our thoughts are like trees. Deep in our roots, we hold core beliefs: blueprints that come from early childhood experiences, often before the age of 10. Core beliefs are simply deeply seated thoughts about ourselves that we acquire in childhood. We often hold onto these beliefs as irrefutable facts. Many times, these thoughts come with intense emotion or affect, for example, being scolded (emotional sadness), falling (physical pain), or bullying (intense self-doubt).

The reality of our core beliefs is that they are not necessarily true; they arise from childhood experiences, from the eyes of a child. Here's an example: here I am, 6 years old, wrapping a present. I do pretty well but make a mess of one of the corners. My father snatches the present away and says: "You don't do anything right." He rewraps it. An objective person might question my father's need to rewrap his six-year-old daughter's present. But as that six-year-old child, here's what I internalize at that moment: *I don't do anything right!*

As a grown woman, with a wall of degrees, I know I do a lot of things right. However, from time to time, in the different roles I play, friend, partner, sister, colleague, professional, something happens to trigger negative thoughts that make me feel like I never do anything right. Back to that tree.

Rising up from the roots, our tree is growing, sprouting branches. Each branch of our tree represents a different role we undertake in our lives. The branches sprout leaves. Each leaf is marked as positive or negative, and these we label as automatic thoughts. As we jump around from branch to branch, we run into these automatic thoughts, both positive and negative. Automatic thoughts are the thoughts that jump around in our *monkey brain* untethered. They can affect our mood, cause physical symptoms, and change the course of our actions by leading us to insecurities and lost opportunities.

We have no problem with the positive thoughts, but negative ones are a whole different story.

For example, my mother says to me: "You forgot my birthday." Or a friend says, "Every time I call you, you're never there!" Or I make dinner and my partner says: "There's too much salt in this dish." At work, I miss a deadline. Guess what automatic thought gets activated from my core beliefs: *I never do anything right*. That's right. So not true in my head, but it feels so true that I give it more power every time it pops up.

Our automatic thoughts trigger deep core beliefs about ourselves, beliefs that we hold onto about ourselves, the world, men, women, money, responsibilities … beliefs that are not necessarily true, but with which we have strong emotional ties. That's one way to frame these deep-seated beliefs about ourselves: automatic thoughts and core beliefs.

As a therapist, I do a lot of work with clients to clean up their automatic thoughts. Here's the good news: when we challenge our automatic thoughts, those core beliefs *automatically* begin to hold less and less value and can even be revised into healthier, adaptive, positive thoughts.

Think about the negative automatic thoughts and core beliefs that you hold. Begin to challenge their veracity.

**SCHEMAS**

Let's talk about schemas. Schemas are maps of information we operate from in our heads. Every time we learn something new, from childhood onwards, we create a schema of it. These maps are useful in helping us navigate the world and deal with the sorting of massive amounts of information.

For example, Lucy starts a new job. On her first day, as she drives to work, she pays attention to the road, the street names, landmarks, and where she turns left and right. She takes care not to make a wrong turn as she makes her way. But once she's driven that route for a week or two, it becomes automatic. By now, weeks later, she's eating breakfast in the car, doing her makeup, talking to friends, singing along to the song on the radio. She no longer needs to pay close attention, because she's operating by using a helpful, positive, and very useful schema. Lucy is running on automatic pilot.

But schemas can also have a downside. An example: the first time Lucy makes dinner reservations for a party of friends, she picks a restaurant, makes a call, and requests a table on the date for the number of people who will be coming for dinner. On the evening of her get-together, she arrives at the restaurant, and requests a table, using her name to let them know she has a reservation. Her party is seated, and they enjoy a pleasant evening. Great schema!

But then, after making restaurant reservations for years, one day, Lucy's on automatic pilot. She makes dinner reservations as usual. But this time, when she shows up with her friends, the restaurant has no record of her reservation! She panics. Her panic situation creates a new schema, a new map in her head, which includes the warning: *Oh my God, what if the reservation gets lost!* It triggers the feeling of a loss of control, which brings on anxiety and activates Lucy's anxiety schema. With it come heart palpitations, sweating palms, and racing negative thoughts. Lucy freezes. She panics and feels a loss of control.

Back to the dilemma of the lost reservation. As her symptoms emerge, Lucy thinks of Plan B: what are the other restaurants in the area? She brings up the maps in her head of the neighborhood and nearby restaurants and remembers a pub across the street and a restaurant a few doors down. Your schemas are not *Google*! They don't have access to everything available. They activate what your knowledge set knows.

Then she thinks of Plan C: *What's in my fridge? Maybe I could cook these people dinner?* Then there's Plan D: Forget it and send everyone home. Since that's no good, Lucy reverts to Plan B. She picks a restaurant just across the street. Her group gets a table and ends up having a wonderful evening.

All's well that ends well, right? Not exactly, because Lucy wakes up the morning after the reservation debacle with emotional debris. Emotional memory of a stressful or unpleasant event is stressful. Confidence in her tried and true restaurant reservation schema has been shattered. The next time she makes dinner reservations, there's a little creeping voice in the back of her mind: *What if this new restaurant also misses my dinner reservation? What do I do?* Lucy develops safety behaviors, things to do that prevent potentially bad things from happening. This type of behavior stems from emotional debris: emotional memories from difficult periods in our life.

Back to Lucy's now fraught task of making a dinner reservation. This time, when she makes dinner reservations, she adds a few new steps to the ones she already knows. Before she shows up for her reservation, she calls several times to confirm that her reservation is in their book. And just to be safe, she makes a couple of backup reservations at a nearby restaurant and the pub across the street, just in case.

I've used a fairly simple example to show how schemas are created and can impact our lives. Here's why we have to pay attention to how schemas develop and play out: when we experience traumas, difficulties, or abuse, we create a map of what relationships look like, what people look like, what men are, what women are, what jobs look like, our communication styles, what our insecurities are, how people treat us, and so on.

We have maps, or schemas, in our heads about every area of our life. Until we record over them, retrace or revisit our maps, we are bound to repeat them. It's why we talk sometimes about turning into our parents. Our parents are our first source of maps about men, women, relationships, love, handling conflict, communication, anger, assertiveness, perfectionism, restlessness, values about religion or spirituality, values about work and re-lationships, and love. Think about the negative experiences in your life that have created emotional debris that led you to develop safety behaviors, ways of avoiding that same negative outcome.

## A THIRD AND FINAL THOUGHT ON THOUGHTS

In this third — and final — aspect of why it's the thought that counts, let's go to a party three times, one scenario, but with three very different thoughts in our heads. Here's an example from *Mind Over Mood*, a CBT workbook by Dennis Greenberger and Christine Padesky.

Take one: we arrive at a party, and I introduce you to Alex. But rather than engage with you in conversation, his eyes dart around the room, looking everywhere but at you. Now, I'm going to give you the thought that runs through your mind, and you choose the mood you think corresponds with that thought. Your thought is: *Alex is rude. He is insulting me by ignoring me.* Would you feel irritated, sad, nervous, or caring in this scenario? Here, most people would feel irritated by Alex's behavior.

Take two: I introduce you to Alex at that same party. Again, he looks everywhere but at you. This time, you have a different thought: *Alex is uninterested in me. No wonder. I bore everyone*. If this were your thought would you feel irritated, sad, nervous, or caring?

Most people would feel sad or nervous in this situation: *Nobody likes me anyway, why bother talking to anyone? I just want to get out of here*. You're feeling sad, uninteresting, and uneasy in this social setting.

Take three: Back at the party, I introduce you to Alex, and again, he pays no attention to you. But this time your thought is: *Alex seems uncomfortable. Maybe he's shy, anxious, or upset about something*. This time, you would most likely feel caring and compassion for Alex.

One scenario with three very different thoughts after meeting Alex ... all that has changed is the perception, interpretation, or thought about a stranger's behavior toward you.

Depending on what thought we pull from thin air, our mood shifts, and so too do our actions and behaviors. The takeaway from the party scenes we just witnessed is that each reaction to Alex's lack of attention was triggered by a thought in your head. You didn't ask Alex: "What's your problem? Why won't you look at me?" If you had, he might have said: "I think I have food poisoning and I need to find a bathroom," or "I'm anxious because I'm worried about my friend, who should have been here an hour ago." People with mood and anxiety disorders tend to pick either thought one or two from our party scene. This is because they are both about them. In psychology, this is what's known as the 'spotlight effect.'

## THE SPOTLIGHT EFFECT

The spotlight effect is when you walk into a room and feel as though all eyes are on you. We become self-conscious and nervous about life when we feel that everyone is noticing everything about us. Here's the interesting reality: everyone has a proverbial screen door of self-consciousness and insecurities. We're all looking at each other through these screen doors wondering if everyone is noticing everything we perceive and believe is wrong about us.

The moment we are in a situation where a negative thought arises, we are not asking for confirmation of our thoughts. We are literally pulling a thought out of midair, or our own schemas and mindsets, giving it life and conducting ourselves accordingly … as though that thought were true. But many times, it is not!

## BEYOND THE SCREEN DOOR OF OUR THOUGHTS

We need to learn to look past that screen door of our thoughts — because just as a screen door lets us see outside, it also diminishes the view, and keeps us from seeing everything as it is. When we do this, we can look at life as though everything is possible. And that allows us to go one step deeper and try to determine the likelihood of any thought being true. Back at that party, each one of those 'thoughts' could have been true. But in real life, we need to develop the ability to determine the likelihood of a specific thought being true. We need to learn to start looking at the screen door of our thoughts. Since everything is possible, we need to explore the probability of something actually *being* true.

Again, self-doubt is just a thought. Why are you putting so much value into a thought that doesn't serve you, help you grow, and make you a better, higher version of yourself? In the exercise at the end of this chapter, you will explore worst-case scenarios and self-doubts.

In this chapter, we've explored the importance of challenging your core beliefs or automatic thoughts, your schemas, and the negative thoughts you pull from thin air. With this information, and through the exercise included in this chapter, you will be able to begin to identify situations that trigger negative thoughts and the behaviors that arise.

To live our highest and best life, we need to challenge our negative thoughts and make our faith bigger than our fear. To that end, I have created a brief exercise to help quiet your mind to examine negative thinking, and challenge the veracity of entrenched negative self-doubts, thoughts, or imagined worst-case scenarios.

We need to learn how to make our faith bigger than our fear. Here's what this means. Fear is self-doubt, not believing your skillset can help you through something. Faith is the exact opposite: believing in your skillset and your capabilities. To date, life has presented you with many tough situations, and you've always dealt with them, right? Even if at times you've felt that you didn't deal with a situation adequately, or in a way you wish you could have, you dealt with it. We don't give ourselves the credit we deserve.

With these new insights around seeing where your thoughts come from, explore your negative beliefs and thoughts about yourself. What are the thoughts that you hold onto that don't serve your highest and best self? What thoughts prevent you from becoming a better version of yourself?

Revisit this chapter and your notes from time to time, anytime you want to go deeper into a situation where your negative thoughts or core beliefs are troubling you. Review the challenges and goals that you set for yourself. What are the next steps that will take you closer to your goal?

Think about it. Our thoughts count because they determine our inner dialogue and affect our self-esteem. Remember, life is just a series of experiences. We can face it and say: "Bring it on!" It's time to move forward and strive to live life as our strongest and best selves. Remember, it's always the thought that counts. We can replace one thought with another.

## EXERCISE

By now you've gained a whole new understanding of why it's the thought that counts, and how negative thoughts can wreak havoc in your life. Take your time to reflect and answer these questions and set the goal of aligning your thoughts to who you want to be and what you want to manifest in your life.

Make a list of any negative automatic thoughts and core beliefs you have about yourself:

## AUTOMATIC THOUGHTS:

_____

_____

_____

_____

_____

CORE BELIEFS:

_____

_____

_____

_____

How do your negative thoughts and self-doubts color your perception of the world, life, people, and yourself?

We all have schemas, or maps, from our upbringing and our positive and negative experiences as we move through life: failures, successes, job losses, relationship breakups, friendships, and more. Take a moment to list the negative experiences in your life that have created emotional debris that led you to develop safety behaviors as ways of avoiding that same negative outcome.

_____

_____

_____

_____

Explore self-doubts and worst-case scenarios. When we are nervous or anxious or inse-cure, we overestimate the likelihood of bad things happening and we end up thinking bad things or worst-case scenarios are very possible. Explore the evidence about the worst-case scenarios you envision. How likely are they?

List situations where you find yourself overestimating the possibility of negative out-comes.

_____

_____

_____

_____

_____

_____

_____

_____

Think about situations in your life where negative core beliefs, schemas, or negative automatic thoughts negatively impact you.

_____

_____

_____

_____

_____

# CHAPTER 5
# UNDERSTANDING THE PURPOSE OF SUFFERING

We all suffer loss, disappointment, failure, and trauma. We all experience pain and hurt. It's part of life. In this chapter, we're going to talk about the purpose of suffering in our lives.

In my practice, I work with many patients who are miserable because of the turmoil, pain, and suffering in their lives. "Why?" they ask, "What is the purpose of all this suffering?" This question comes up time and time again. At spiritual talks or retreats, people ask the Dalai Lama and other respected spiritual leaders the same question: "Why do we suffer?"

Understanding the purpose of suffering is of critical importance because truly understanding it enables us to regain the power we feel we have lost when we experience pain and suffering.

## A SERIES OF EXPERIENCES

We know from our previous work that life is a series of experiences, and we judge and label these experiences as positive or negative. In everyone's life, there are positives and negatives. For us to appreciate the richness of a good moment in our lives, we need to have the polar opposite — the negative.

A perfect example is found in the M. Night Shyamalan film, *Unbreakable*. As the film begins, security guard David Dunn, played by Bruce Willis, the sole survivor of a horrific train wreck, walks away miraculously unharmed. News of his survival catches the attention of Elijah Price (played by Samuel L. Jackson), a wheelchair-bound comic store owner. He is Dunn's polar opposite: fragile and frail, with a rare genetic disorder that causes his bones to break easily. He is so fragile that turning a doorknob can break his wrist. Price meets Dunn and they speak of opposites, good versus evil, weak versus strong. Price says: "If there's someone like me in the world, and I'm at one end of the spectrum, couldn't there be someone else, the opposite of me at the other end?" In that moment, Dunn, the unbreakable man, realizes that he is face to face with his polar opposite, the easily breakable Elijah Price.

The message in this story is that we all have opposites in our life. The difficult times teach us to have gratitude for the good times. We need to develop a deeper understanding of suffering. Why? Because when we accurately understand the purpose of suffering, we become better at dealing with it. The first step to understanding and treatment is awareness, and awareness comes from recognizing the power of our thoughts. It is through our thoughts that we can begin to see suffering in a new light.

We all have suffering, pain, sorrow, hurts, painful and devastating break-ups, job losses, and illnesses. Terrible things can happen: accidents, natural disasters, traumas, abuse, and losses. Anxiety and depression are some of the symptoms that come when we encounter pain and suffering.

As we move through suffering, it intensifies, becomes worse and worse. Our symptoms become more intense. As we suffer, our symptoms get louder and louder, and more painful. Here, the true purpose of suffering reveals itself: suffering is a catalyst for change! Suffering propels us to shift and change, to learn a new skillset, and to move closer to becoming our highest and best self. We do the best we can with what we have, and suffering propels us to learn skills to be better versions of ourselves.

If we didn't feel discomfort or experience suffering and pain in our lives, we would never change. As suffering comes into our lives, it leads us forward by being a catalyst for change. It compels us to acquire new skillsets, build resilience and strength, discover new opportunities, and unearth untapped potential.

**In the exercise at the end of this chapter, you'll explore your past hurts, what you may have personalized from these experiences, and how your pain has been a catalyst for change in your life.**

## A CATALYST FOR CHANGE

Here's an example of suffering as a catalyst for positive change. There's a restructuring in management at the company where I have worked diligently, happily, and successfully for 10 years. My boss is assigned to a new role. Now I have a new boss and a new role with added responsibilities. I struggle with this new boss. I am getting more and more work dumped on me. I feel unappreciated and no longer valued. I begin feeling an inner conflict. I'm dragging my feet to go to work, experiencing low mood and anxiety, and feeling upset with my new boss. My symptoms get louder and louder by the day. They intensify with each negative development and unpleasant encounter until one day there comes the moment that is the catalyst for change. I finally say to myself: *Enough! I deserve better. I'm going to take my skillset and go somewhere where I'll be appreciated*.

My suffering has become a catalyst for change that propels me forward to the place where I am meant to go. I would never have looked for a new job if it wasn't for that pain and suffering.

In the aftermath of my suffering, it is important to let go of the emotional debris, to not carry the suffering of my former situation into the present or future, into my next job or relationship, for example. Instead, we need to forgive and release our pain by saying something like: *I release or forgive my difficult boss, as this person came into my life to teach me and help me see my value and my skillset as valuable and underappreciated. It compelled me to go elsewhere, to seek and find a better and higher place for me to be happy and grow*.

Let's look at another not uncommon and often very painful example: the break-up of a relationship.

Sam is in a romantic relationship. He's suffering and in pain because he is feeling unappreciated, unloved, and unvalued. As his symptoms intensify, he begins to realize what a horrible relationship he is in, and he feels stuck. He's sad, angry, and depressed all day every day, and feeling lost and empty. Sam's feelings lead him to a place of change. His suffering becomes a catalyst for change. And his unhappy relationship teaches him to make himself a priority in his life, to put himself ahead of other people, in short, to love himself more than he loves the habit of being with someone. Things shift and change, and we need to allow ourselves to embrace these shifts and feel capable of dealing with them. We need to begin to believe that change is good. In retrospect, most often, the fear of change is worse than the change itself.

We sometimes love other people at the expense of ourselves. But when the suffering is bad enough, we put ourselves first, and realize that we deserve better, and leave a bad relationship and move on, because we deserve better.

Moving on is about releasing your pain rather than carrying it with you. It's about forgiving or releasing a negative relationship. You can make a declaration to yourself:

> *I release (or forgive) this relationship as it caused me a lot of pain and suffering and left me feeling unappreciated and not feeling the love I deserve. It taught me to walk away from whatever is not serving me, not making me happy. It also taught me to stand up for myself, set boundaries, and walk away from someone hurtful in my life. This relationship has taught me to be a better person and to strive to be my highest and best self.*

Once you act on a change, it is important to let go of the emotional memory of the story of the pain that brought us to that change by understanding that the pain came to us as a lesson for us to learn and change, and grow into our highest and best self. In our suffering, we often don't recognize the need to change. Instead, we personalize and hold onto the experience. When we do this, we stay stuck. When we're stuck, we repeat patterns over and over.

Examine your past hurts and understand your suffering through a new lens. Think about some of the major pain and sorrows and hurts you've experienced in the past. Reflect on how the pain you suffered acted as a catalyst for change in your life.

We often don't recognize the positive changes that suffering brings into our lives. We personalize — and hold onto — a painful, negative experience, and stay stuck. Not believing in our skillset to manage or move forward, we repeat negative patterns over and over. When we don't have faith in ourselves, when we don't believe in ourselves, we repeat patterns. We say: "I'm too scared," and stay in that bad relationship or bad job for another five years … or until that pain and suffering gets louder and louder, to the point where we realize that we need to change.

Is there a situation in your current life that is causing you pain and suffering? Is it part of a pattern that is repeating itself?

**RESISTING CHANGE**

We need to recognize that if a pattern is repeating in our life, we're resisting change, and we're choosing instead to stay stuck in something familiar rather than taking the chance that there will be something good in the change that comes forth. Another reason we're afraid of change harkens back to our schemas.

Schemas, you'll recall, are entrenched beliefs and insights about yourself, others, and how events and situations will play out. Many of our schemas are formed early in our lives and become automatic. On the plus side, schemas help us make sense of the world. On the minus, they can limit our thoughts and prevent us from taking in new information or considering new possibilities.

For example, many of us were raised to think of change as something to fear and avoid if at all possible. But change can be beautiful: a new home, a new baby, a new relationship, a proposal, or a new job or career change with a raise. There can be wonderful surprises.

We can become afraid of change on an emotional memory front due to painful experiences, such as a job loss, illness or death of a loved one, relationship break-ups, abuse, feeling victimized, or living through a trauma or disaster.

Sometimes we fear change because we link it to negative experiences, such as money loss, emotional torment, physical suffering, or grief. But the truth is there are beautiful things that come with change: new relationships, healthier environments, appreciation, career advancement, challenging yourself to be a stronger, deeper, better, and more compassionate version of yourself.

The purpose of suffering is to help us to grow and shift to be our highest and best self in life. We stop growing if we resist change. When you experience suffering and pain and you're not happy where you are, you can take a step forward to get to a better place. Whether it's a relationship, a workplace, new friends, or cutting out old friends, when we are stuck in fear and self-doubt, we get stuck in maladaptive patterns and stay there longer, and prolong our suffering.

**TIME TO SET A GOAL**

When you are in pain, it's important to recognize that it's time to set a goal. Where there is suffering in your life, it forces you to think about where you would rather be. Your pain is an opportunity for growth and change for your betterment. Every time something painful shows up in your life, ask yourself: *What is this trying to show me? How am I supposed to grow? What is it teaching me? What is it forsing me to see that I need to learn in order to become my highest and best self and have a happier life?*

Explore how you can support positive changes in your life. Examine your suffering. How is it trying to help you change? Ask yourself: *What are the changes trying to bring for my highest and best self? How many things am I carrying right now that I should be forgiving and letting go? What is the purpose of holding on?* Don't assume isolated negative events will be never-ending patterns.

Our purpose in life is to create interest for ourselves. As human beings, we are propelled to learn, grow and evolve. We learn a lot of lessons and we make a lot of changes as we go through life. But often we keep a lot of our most painful stories alive in ourselves by personalizing stories or events that were hurtful experiences. We are not meant to personalize our pain. We are meant to learn from it, grow from it, and move ahead to live in the present moment.

**In the exercise at the end of this chapter, you'll develop strategies for moving past pain to create meaningful change in your life and lighten the emotional load you carry within.**

Start looking at your suffering in a new way. When we realize its true purpose, we can use it as a means of release from situations that no longer serve us. Then we can begin to move toward building a stronger, better life for ourselves.

People often say this is easier said than done. But remember, as kids we were not negative. As we move through life, we acquire negative states, self-critical perspectives, and doubts. Let's put choices in place that work in our favor rather than sticking with what keeps us stuck. Decide to put your suffering to good use as a catalyst for positive change and growth.

It's time to make a commitment to yourself by setting a concrete goal toward positive change. As you begin to understand the purpose of suffering and learn to move beyond it to create change in your life, that change is a process with challenges and rewards. Allow yourself time, patience, and compassion to work toward your goal.

Return to this lesson anytime you find yourself mired in past pain and suffering. Review the challenges and goals that you set for yourself here today. Ask yourself how much closer to your goals you are today than when you began. What are the next steps that will take you closer to your goal? Use this lesson and your notes to reinforce your commitment to change, to reset your goals and strategies, and to work through any new situations that are causing you pain and suffering.

## EXERCISE

Make a list of some of the major pain and hurts you've experienced in the past.

Think about how the pain you suffered acted as a catalyst for change for you. How has a past hurt helped you shift and grow to be a better, healthier version of yourself?

_____

_____

_____

_____

_____

_____

_____

_____

_____

_____

_____

_____

_____

_____

_____

_____

_____

Is there a situation in your life right now that is causing you major pain? If so, make a list of potential actions you could take to diminish current suffering in your life, and see what you are personalizing and what is holding you back.

# CHAPTER 6
# UNDERSTANDING ANXIETY
# AND THE CYCLE OF PANIC

We all struggle with change. Change brings some uncomfortable feelings. In previous chapters, we've talked about how making meaningful, positive changes in our lives takes commitment and, at times, painful reflection and the courage to challenge long-held beliefs about ourselves, our abilities, and our limitations. We've explored the symptoms that arise when we have problems in our lives with work, intimacy, self-care, and spirituality. In this chapter, we're going to explore anxiety and the cycle of panic, and how we can manage the situations where our fear becomes stronger than our faith. Let's begin.

When we're in a situation or setting that makes us anxious, our feelings of discomfort begin to rise, increasing our anxiety, and can lead to a state of panic. Often, we are faced with navigating through change. Change is not easy. It fosters uncertainty and fear and triggers intense feelings of self-doubt. We become unsure of ourselves and frightened, which leads to an intense feeling of panic about our ability to cope with what's going on. As a sense of dread creeps in, it can trigger thoughts of potential worst-case scenarios and catastrophic outcomes. This can culminate in a panic state, what's commonly known as a panic attack. I am going to break down the cycle of panic so you can understand the unhealthy cycle that can develop when you're nervous and anxious.

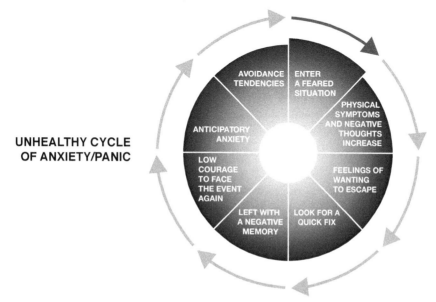

**UNHEALTHY CYCLE OF ANXIETY/PANIC**

AVOIDANCE TENDENCIES

ENTER A FEARED SITUATION

PHYSICAL SYMPTOMS AND NEGATIVE THOUGHTS INCREASE

ANTICIPATORY ANXIETY

FEELINGS OF WANTING TO ESCAPE

LOW COURAGE TO FACE THE EVENT AGAIN

LEFT WITH A NEGATIVE MEMORY

LOOK FOR A QUICK FIX

I like to use this circle to illustrate what the cycle of panic looks like, and how it works. We all face feared, dreaded, and even panic-invoking situations. When you enter into an anxiety-provoking situation — social, work-related, a relationship confrontation, or a feared setting, such as an elevator, driving on a busy highway, flying, or water — the first thing that alerts you to the fact that you're in an uncomfortable situation is that you begin to experience an increase in physiological (physical) symptoms. As these symptoms — which may include heart palpitations, sweating, mind racing, abdominal discomfort, or fatigue — begin to increase in intensity, your thoughts start racing, you start ruminating, thinking the same negative thoughts and imagining the same worst-case scenarios over and over again.

## UNDERSTANDING THE CYCLE OF PANIC

Let's follow the cycle of panic around the circle.

Imagine yourself in a feared or anxiety-provoking situation. Your physical symptoms increase. Negative thoughts start racing in your head. The first thing you want to do when you're feeling panicky is to escape, get out of there, find a safety zone. But if your feared situation is your office Holiday party, a company board meeting, a class, the dentist, writing an exam, or taking the driver's road test, chances are you can't leave. It's just not an option.

What do most of us do in a panic situation, something from which we cannot escape? We look for a quick fix: a cigarette break or nerve-calming alcohol or drugs, such as Ativan, lorazepam, or cannabis. Another quick fix might be a brief retreat to the washroom for a break, a moment alone to take a few deep breaths, and maybe splash water on your face. We look for distractions as quick fixes as well: a colleague, a pal, a friendly face, a place to briefly step back from what's happening.

What's so wrong with reaching for that quick fix? After using whatever quick fix we've managed to find to help endure an uncomfortable situation and lessen distress, we end up with a negative memory; and with that negative memory comes decreased self-confidence to handle the next situation in which we do not feel in complete control. This memory creates a mindset known as anticipatory anxiety.

## ANTICIPATORY ANXIETY

Anticipatory anxiety is an interesting one. The first time you have anxiety in your life, it takes a long time for your anxiety to peak. After that first negative experience, each time you encounter that situation — even just as a thought — those feelings build and become very intense, very quickly. This sets the stage for an anxiety attack.

For example, I've been riding in elevators without a second thought all my life. But after reading a couple of tragic news stories about deadly elevator mishaps, one day I get a little panicky in an old, overcrowded elevator that stalls between floors a couple of times. I begin feeling uneasy and claustrophobic, and by the time I arrive at my floor, my heart is racing. I am relieved when I step out into the hallway. The first time I panic in an elevator, it takes a lot of time for my feelings to peak.

Later that evening, I'm home and I'm safe and watching an old movie on TV, and all of a sudden George Clooney is making out with a girl in an elevator. Just watching this scene raises my anxiety. I'm relaxing on my couch, safe and sound, but the mere sight of an elevator spikes my anxiety and sends me into a mild panic.

## HIGH ANXIETY

Once you experience that first cycle of panic in a specific situation or setting, your panic cycle becomes shorter and shorter, and even brief thoughts can trigger that anxiety, and lead to overwhelming anticipatory anxiety in an imagined feared situation. This can lead to a very ugly place called avoidance.

When this happens, we start cutting things that bring us anxiety out of our lives. We don't want to face a situation in real life when the mere thought of it makes us anxious. Think about the anxiety-provoking situations in your life and the avoidance behaviors you've utilized to prevent having to confront your anxieties.

Let's explore how the cycle of anxiety plays out and what a healthy way of dealing with panic looks like. You find yourself in a feared, anxiety-provoking situation. You are anxious and uncomfortable. Maybe it's a situation you've avoided for so long that you're simply out of practice as to how to deal with it. But this time, instead of avoiding it, you choose to stay in the situation and ride it out. Dealing with anxiety and panic-provoking situations is just like exercising a muscle. The more you exercise your arms, the stronger your arm muscles become. Many of the situations that cause us anxiety are situations that we haven't really repeated or exercised often enough, so our 'muscle' becomes a little bit weaker. You need to use it more. You need to set the goal of becoming bored, unbothered by, and comfortable with whatever is making you anxious. Repeat until boredom with whatever triggers your anxiety sets in.

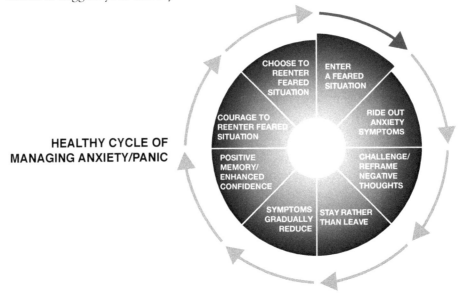

**HEALTHY CYCLE OF MANAGING ANXIETY/PANIC**

- CHOOSE TO REENTER FEARED SITUATION
- ENTER A FEARED SITUATION
- RIDE OUT ANXIETY SYMPTOMS
- CHALLENGE/REFRAME NEGATIVE THOUGHTS
- STAY RATHER THAN LEAVE
- SYMPTOMS GRADUALLY REDUCE
- POSITIVE MEMORY/ENHANCED CONFIDENCE
- COURAGE TO REENTER FEARED SITUATION

## A HEALTHY CYCLE

Here's what a healthy cycle looks like. You're in it, but you don't leave or reach for that quick fix. Instead, you pay attention to your feelings and thoughts. You watch for an increase in physical symptoms and racing thoughts. The moment this starts to happen, you practice rolling with your anxiety. You bring in some deep breathing and create other physical grounding practices (like closing your eyes for a few seconds or counting backward from 10 to 1) to prevent yourself from getting carried away by negative thoughts. The goal here is to feel a little bit more grounded in your body and relaxed as your mind starts racing and your physical symptoms intensify. Connecting to our senses allows us to ground ourselves. Smell a scent, taste candy, take a deep breath, feel a cool breeze, take in details, touch different textures, jump up and down. Try anything to connect through your senses back to yourself, in the present.

**CHALLENGING NEGATIVE THOUGHTS**

About the negative thoughts that give rise to panic, you need to learn how to challenge them. Rather than sticking with the catastrophic scenarios playing out in your head, thoughts that you hold onto from past negative experiences, worst-case scenarios that you've pulled from thin air and given life, you can begin to challenge, revise, and examine them in realistic terms.

**In the exercise at the end of this chapter, you'll have an opportunity to identify situations in your life that cause you anxiety and choose a specific situation that you would like to address. And best of all — you'll be able to create actionable strategies to help you conquer your anxieties.**

**WHAT GOES UP…**

When it comes to physical symptoms, what goes up must come down. Imagine yourself in an anxiety-provoking situation. As you're breathing deeply, you're sitting with uncomfortable feelings, and allowing your anxiety level to come down. Remember, what goes up must come down. Your symptoms are going to pass either way. Nothing is static; everything shifts and changes. But, when you acknowledge your thoughts and feelings and mindfully calm yourself down, they'll pass more quickly than if you avoid them and shut out your emotions.

As you experience your physical symptoms and you're rolling with them, you're also challenging some of those negative thoughts, rather than escaping, by resisting the natural inclination to flee. You instead choose to remain mindfully in the situation. Gradually, you experience symptom reduction. You will find that what goes up is indeed coming down. Before you know it, you get a little calmer. Your physical symptoms subside, and your negative thoughts start to slow down in intensity and rumination.

Riding out a feared experience gives you the courage to say: "Hey, I handled that." You have also created a somewhat positive memory, which leaves you with a sense of some confidence, and reduces anticipatory anxiety because you did it! This allows you to have the courage to intentionally enter the feared situation again. Psychologists call practicing riding out uncomfortable situations *exposure therapy*. The more you do something the easier it becomes and the better you get at it. Remember, the goal of exposure therapy is to become bored by what makes you anxious.

## OVERCOMING FEAR THROUGH REPETITION

There is one highly successful approach when it comes to overcoming anxiety and panic: learning to master whatever makes you anxious. Ride out a situation that makes you anxious, then repeat it until you are bored by it. And how do you get bored with anything? You do it over and over and over again. If you're afraid of dating, become a lean, mean dating machine. Arrange several dates a week. If you're worried about public speaking, join a club, such as *Toastmasters*, where you'll be speaking in front of others three or four times a week.

## RULES OF EXPOSURE

With situations that make us anxious, we need to take charge and learn how to get bored by what makes us anxious by repeating it until we feel more capable and confident. When it comes to exposure therapy, here are a few winning strategies:

Exposure Therapy:

- Needs to be gradual. Take baby steps to gain confidence. Be careful not to recreate situations that deepen your anxiety and set you into a state of panic. Flooding is a term referring to going into a situation that is too hard. It can leave you feeling traumatized and hopeless. Exposures need to be gradual and incremental.
- Needs to be prolonged. You want to remain in the exposure environment for more than 15 minutes; with longer exposure you allow a new experience to sink in and become a pattern.
- Needs to be repeated. You have to do it three to five times a week. If you do something only once or twice a week, it will always feel like a new task. The more you do something, the stronger that muscle becomes.

Recognize how you can gain control by riding out situations that cause you anxiety, discomfort, and panic. Understand and realize that you can shift. Make your faith and belief in your skillset bigger than your fear. Powerful strategies such as managing physical symptoms through breathing or grounding practices, challenging negative thoughts by examining the evidence that supports and sustains your worst-case scenarios, and practicing exposure therapy in feared situations, will bolster self-confidence and create positive memories that mitigate anticipatory anxiety.

Allow your faith in your skillset to override your anxieties and self-doubts. Remember that your fears and self-doubts are only thoughts. Through more positive and empowering thoughts and actions, you can regain your power and control.

As you begin to create meaningful changes in your life, allow yourself time, patience, and compassion to work toward your goals. And remember that reinforcement strengthens our determination and commitment. Revisit this chapter and its lessons from time to time. Reread your notes about the challenges that you have identified, and the strategies and goals that you set for yourself to overcome them. Ask yourself how much closer to your goal are you today than when you began. What are the next steps that will take you closer to your goal?

You can use this lesson time and time again to reinforce your commitment to change, reset your goals and strategies, and work through situations in your life that cause you anxiety.

## EXERCISE

Identify your sources of anxiety. Think about the situations in your life where you feel anxiety and panic, a serious and troubling fear. List them.

_____

_____

_____

_____

_____

_____

_____

_____

_____

_____

From this list, choose one that impacts your life significantly that you would like to conquer. Consider your worst-case scenario in this situation. In as much detail as you can, describe your imagined worst-case, or feared, outcome.

_____

_____

_____

_____

_____

_____

--------------------------------------------------

--------------------------------------------------

--------------------------------------------------

--------------------------------------------------

--------------------------------------------------

--------------------------------------------------

--------------------------------------------------

--------------------------------------------------

--------------------------------------------------

--------------------------------------------------

Explore the evidence that your imagined worst-case scenario is going to unfold. Is this really possible? Is this really probable (anything might be possible)? How likely is this to happen to you?

--------------------------------------------------

--------------------------------------------------

--------------------------------------------------

--------------------------------------------------

--------------------------------------------------

Now, imagine yourself experiencing a positive outcome in the same situation. How would it play out? How would you feel?

_____

_____

_____

_____

_____

_____

_____

_____

_____

_____

_____

_____

_____

_____

_____

_____

_____

_____

List the situations or settings in your life where repeated exposures could help alleviate your anxiety. Create a list of exposure activities to address what is making you anxious, activities that you would like to master. You are highly likely to succeed when you are highly motivated to conquer whatever is making you anxious.

_____

_____

_____

_____

_____

_____

_____

_____

_____

_____

_____

_____

_____

_____

_____

_____

_____

_____

# CHAPTER 7
# COMMUNICATION

We're born alone and we die alone. Our journey is about learning to be a better version of ourselves. For you to be a better version of yourself, you have to learn how to communicate with yourself, in truth.

We're going to go deeper. And it's all about you. We're going to talk about communication, and how improving communication — with ourselves, which then leads to improved communication with others — can help facilitate positive changes in our lives. We need to learn how to facilitate change in our lives by learning to communicate well, not only with others but, most importantly, with ourselves. It all starts with you. Before you can get it right with others, you need to get right within yourself.

This chapter is all about communication. We'll explore why the most important person we need to learn how to communicate with is ourselves. You'll learn valuable strategies and tools, and how to set goals to support positive changes in your life. Most patients I see talk a great deal about anger. So let's start there.

## A BAD REPUTATION

Anger has a really bad reputation as violent, explosive, and dangerous. Each and every one of us has a version of anger that we display to people. Some of us turn anger inward, which can lead to depression and self-harm. Most of us would like to know how to deal with our anger, but we have virtually no understanding of it. Understanding anger is all about breaking down what is underneath the anger.

Anger, it turns out, is pretty simple to break down.

What is really happening when we're upset with someone? When we are upset with someone, what is really going on is that the person we are upset with is reflecting our uncomfortable feelings or sensations of feeling insecure, incompetent, or not good enough. People are just mirroring back our own sensations, judgments, views, and experiences.

Every person we interact with is showing us a mirror of ourselves. Each situation and every person we meet reflects certain traits or qualities about ourselves back to us. For example, Monica knows who she is as a daughter in front of her mother. She knows who she is as a partner in front of her partner, a sibling in front of her brother, a student in front of a textbook, in winter in winter, in summer in summer. The world outside teaches us how we are in various roles, events, experiences, and situations. What do we do when we get angry? We spill over onto others. We blame other people for our anger, but others are not making us angry. It's our communication and our interpretation of what's going on that's making us angry. We first see something that, with our insecurities, we judge negatively. This, in turn, causes us unpleasant emotions that lead us to inward and/or outward anger.

Happy, sad, nervous, and scared: these are *blanket words*, meaning they cover a lot of ground, but don't give us a clear picture of what's going on in our mind, body, and emotions, or the outer world. Anger is also a blanket word. Most people demonize anger, they misinterpret it, personalize it, and categorize it as extreme. Anger, as a blanket word, doesn't reveal the depth of what someone in a state of anger is actually going through. Neither does it reveal the clear and true story of the real emotions hidden beneath the blanket of anger.

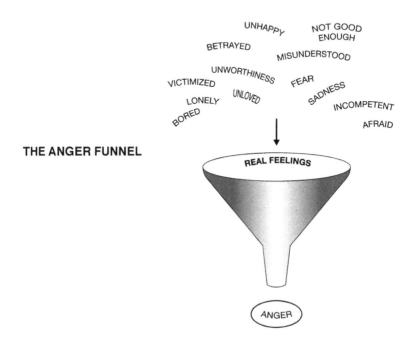

We can use this funnel to break down anger into its real feelings. What are the real feelings going on underneath or behind your anger? Anger can stem from many things, such as love, sadness, feeling embarrassed, feeling a loss of control, feeling irritated, sad, lonely, dependent, embarrassed, incompetent, or incapable. Anger can stem from feeling guilty, victimized, bored, frustrated, powerless, irate, betrayed, taken advantage of, unlovable, loss of control, lost, scared, or frightened. Anger can stem from all of these feelings and more.

We need to explore our anger and break it down to understand what is really going on. What are the real feelings behind my anger? People around you are not making you angry. Your feelings of insecurity are the true source of your anger.

Let's explore how anger looks and changes at various stages in life. For example, Mary, at 27, goes online to start dating. She meets Keith. They arrange to meet in person and have a wonderful evening. They go on a second date. That date also goes well and at the end of the evening, Keith says, "Tomorrow I'll give you a call."

Let's go back in time here to Mary's childhood. Her father used to say to her, "Hey, Mary, when you spit on the ground, do you ever lick it back up?" She would answer, "No, that's gross!" He'd add, "So when you say you're going to do something, it is like spitting. You don't lick it back up, you do it." So, Mary was brought up with the core value: *when you say you're going to do something, you do it*. Mary expects this not only from herself but from everybody else who comes into her life.

Back to Keith and Mary at 27. It's the day after their second date, and Mary's waiting for Keith's call. But the phone doesn't ring. So Mary gets angry. Let's look at what Mary's anger is really all about.

**MARY'S ANGER FUNNEL, AGE 27**

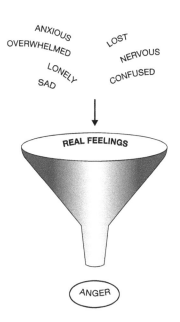

She's feeling insecure that Keith has maybe met somebody else. She's feeling lonely, sad that he didn't call, let down, lost, confused, overwhelmed. She's feeling nervous and anxious. Realizing that Keith is just some guy she's only been on two dates with, she shakes off her feelings and lets them go.

Five months later, Mary and Keith are still dating. She's shared the core value that she learned as a child: *If you make a promise and say you're going to do something, you always follow through.* One evening, Keith tells Mary he's going out with the guys and promises he will call her later when he returns home. But he doesn't call, and Mary gets angry as she stays up waiting for this call into the wee hours.

This time her anger stems from a different place — from feeling unheard. She's feeling insecure, wondering whether the reason he hasn't called is that he's met another girl. She's feeling forgotten, invisible, like she doesn't matter. She's feeling taken for granted, as if she's not setting proper boundaries, and is stupid, incompetent, and naïve. She feels doubt about Keith's integrity and feelings for her. Maybe he's not the right guy and she's worried that she's putting all this time and energy into someone who is going to break her heart.

**MARY'S ANGER FUNNEL, 5 MONTHS IN**

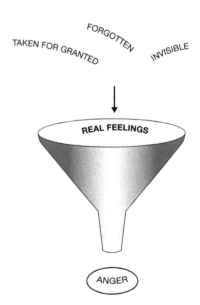

Fast forward another five years. Keith and Mary are married with two young children. One night Keith announces that he is going out with the guys and will call when he's on his way home. Again, Keith forgets to make that promised call.

Again, Mary finds herself angry. But this time underneath her anger she is feeling unheard, anxious, and scared. She plays out worst-case scenarios in her head, imagining her husband dead on the street with her having no way of knowing how to find him. She's thinking of how much she loves him, and if something happened how would she and the kids survive without him. She scolds herself for being silly, and is frustrated with herself for being unable to conquer her anxiety and insecurity. Fearful of worst-case scenarios, she cannot fall asleep.

Then Keith walks through the door. Mary's in a rage, but if she shows her anger, she knows Keith will get defensive and they will get into an argument.

Instead, she lets him know she's angry, but that she's not angry with him. She explains that when she doesn't know where he is and he doesn't call as promised, her mind goes to fearful places and leaves her feeling, afraid, insecure, lost. She wonders whether something bad has happened to him and worries about how dependent she and the children are on him. Her mind goes to such dark places that she can't settle herself down and get to sleep, even though he is more likely than not just being his sometimes absent-minded self and has simply forgotten all about his promise to call her.

**MARY'S ANGER FUNNEL, MID-30's**

SCARED · ANXIOUS · SAD · PLAYED OUT WORST-CASE SCENARIOS

REAL FEELINGS

ANGER

If, like Mary, we can take ownership of what's going on inside when we're angry, the person we're angry with can begin to understand what is really going on rather than simply reacting to our anger and becoming defensive. The moment you say, "I'm angry with you," that person takes it as an attack and they become defensive and begin to defend themselves rather than hearing why you're upset.

To better communicate with others, the first person you need to communicate with is yourself. What's the mirror going on between you and the person who is 'making' you angry? What are you truly feeling on the inside? Remember, anger — like nervousness, sadness, and anxiety — is just a blanket word. It covers a lot of ground without giving proper context to what is going on.

**In the exercise at the end of this chapter, you will have the opportunity to work on breaking down your anger and discovering the real feelings underneath.**

## ANGER TOWARD OTHER PEOPLE

We can also do this with people in mind. I can place someone who I struggle with in the bubble at the bottom of the funnel and ask myself: what traits of this person do I like? What are the traits that I share? What traits do I have trouble with? Remember, in our interactions with other people, they act as a mirror. This whole story is about you. In our lives, we bring people in, and we, at times, push them away. And every single person we encounter teaches us something about ourselves. This mirror helps us grow. Here's an example. Let's discover what is revealed as Mary puts her feelings about her mother, who she struggles with at times, through the funnel. Mary really wants to figure out what's happening in the ongoing struggles between her and her mother. So she puts her mother in the bubble at the bottom of the funnel. Then she makes note of the real feelings that she associates with her mother.

### MARY'S 'MOTHER' FUNNEL

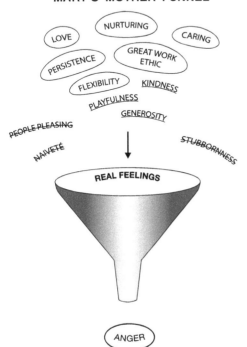

There's a lot of love there. There's also nurturance and caring. Mary recognizes admirable qualities in her mother, such as persistence, a great work ethic, playfulness, flexibility, kindness, and generosity. She also notes qualities of her mother that frustrate her: a tendency to overextend herself, her people-pleasing nature, her stubbornness, her naïveté, and her tendency to be easily influenced by others. Mary circles the traits she likes and admires, underlines the ones she shares, and crosses off the ones she does not share with her mother or is frustrated or irritated with.

Chances are if you find traits you admire in others, you probably share the same traits or aspire to attain these traits. After all, we are mirrors for each other. In Mary's case, generosity, kindness, and playfulness are very nice traits to share with another person.

The qualities she dislikes and crosses off are ones she doesn't share or shares but does not like in herself. These traits she struggles with.

## MIRROR, MIRROR

Here's what we can learn from Mary's exercise: everyone in our lives is a mirror reflecting aspects of ourselves to us. Each person we meet and interact with shows us different aspects of ourselves. When we build awareness of our own traits and those of the people around us, we can then begin to relate to them, rather than lashing out and reacting. We can say to ourselves: *Hey, there's a lot of things about this person that I love or admire. And as for the things I struggle with — they're not their fault. They're just traits I don't share. I struggle with them because I can't relate to them or do not know how to manage, react to, or deal with them.*

Remember, when someone mirrors back a trait — not necessarily a 'bad' one — with which you struggle or cannot relate, you need to reflect on what you need to do to approach that trait with loving kindness and compassion. This is the path to dealing more effectively and compassionately with problematic characteristics and qualities in others.

The world outside of us — including the people in it — is just showing us sides of ourselves so that we can become better, higher, and more authentic versions of ourselves. When we meet people we see as better than us, we have the opportunity to grow. We can strive to become more like what we admire in them by understanding and embodying what we admire about them. And that's why we're here — to become better, higher versions of ourselves.

**In the exercise at the end of this chapter, you'll have a chance to explore the traits of a person you struggle with in your life.**

## WHAT GOES AROUND...

Let's talk about Karma. We've all heard the adage, *What goes around, comes around*, and we all know that negativity just leads to more negativity. When we're in low self-esteem and pain, we personalize the behaviors of others. We react and our pain and negativity spill out onto others.

For example, if my mother swears at me, and I'm in low self-esteem, I might react by swearing back at her. All of a sudden, we are both reacting negatively, and the situation can devolve into a very bad one in no time. In extreme cases, when negativity multiplies and builds, interactions can end in violence.

But if, when my mother swears at me, I am working on being my higher and better self, I understand that she is in a place of pain or stuck in unhealthy, maladaptive habits or patterns from her past. What should I do instead? In short, I need to respond, rather than react. Responding involves practicing the pause, reflecting, and revising a negative reaction to a positive, thought-out response. If I hug her, I break the cycle of negativity. With this more compassionate response, anger and negativity can no longer grow. And just maybe we can both move into a place of being more positive with each other.

Here's an example of acting and reacting out in the world we can all relate to — shopping in a grocery store. Gina, a busy and overburdened working mother, out shopping at Costco after work, is lined up with other shoppers and their oversized carts for a sample of a dumpling. The woman in the cart ahead of Gina takes her sample, pops it into her mouth, and throws her toothpick and napkin onto the floor. The woman working the sample station requests loudly for the woman who has thrown her garbage on the floor to please come back and pick it up. The shopper ignores her request and just walks away.

The Costco employee becomes upset, steps out from behind her table, picks up the toothpick and napkin and puts them in the wastebasket while complaining aloud that it's not her job to clean up after others. Gina approaches the woman and apologizes on the other customer's behalf. This only further saddens and upsets the sample woman, who complains to Gina that she is treated the same way at home and by her friends. No one respects her. No one appreciates what she does, so she shouldn't be surprised when here at work random strangers walking by treat her the same way.

At this point, Gina could just grab her dumpling and be on her way. But she sees that the woman behind the table is in pain, so she approaches her and says, "Hey, you're doing a great job. I really appreciate you, and just because some people take you for granted, please know you are a good person to be who you are. I'd like to give you a hug if you are okay with it." Reluctantly, the sample woman agrees to let Gina hug her. As they embrace, Gina thanks her for what she is doing, tells her again that she is doing a great job, and whispers, "Don't let anyone dull your shine." Gina smiles and her own state of mind shifts from despair and feeling worthless to feeling better about herself. And maybe the grocery store employee can forgive those who take her for granted, who may, themselves, be in low self-esteem.

The employee wishes Gina a good evening, and they part, both feeling better as a result of Gina's compassionate response to a person in pain.

## CHALLENGE YOUR ANGER

When you explore the feelings beneath the blanket emotion of anger, you begin to understand what these people and situations are mirroring back to you, and you can then communicate more authentically and compassionately with yourself and others. You can put forth positive, energizing emotions rather than negative, depleting ones.

To better communicate with ourselves and others, we need to delve deeper into our own feelings to understand ourselves. As we strive to make changes that move us into being our highest and best selves, we need to learn to slow down and take the time to reflect on our own feelings.

**In the exercise at the end of this chapter, you'll have the opportunity to think about the people or situations that trigger anger with which you struggle, and consider potential actions you could take to explore the feelings behind your anger, to interpret them accurately, and act accordingly to produce a healthier response.**

## MEANINGFUL CHANGE IN YOUR LIFE

As you begin to better communicate with yourself and others in your life, you will begin to have healthier, more supportive interactions with friends, family members, colleagues, and perhaps even your employer. Likewise, you will find yourself challenged, as it is not always easy. Among friends, family members, and colleagues you are likely to find potential saboteurs, non-supportive individuals who are threatened by your commitment to change. There will be overwhelming work, family, and social obligations that threaten to weaken your resolve. You may be discouraged by small setbacks, self-sabotaging settings, situations, and individuals, or a lack of peer support. Positive changes, like other healthy commitments, require consistency and determination. Wobbles are normal; don't get discouraged, and get back on track if you slip back to reacting instead of responding one day.

Take a good look at the people in your life, and the environments in which you work, live, and play. Where do you anticipate running into difficulties while making the changes you want to make? Where in your life will you find support as you move toward your goals?

## TIME TO GO DEEPER

One of the main reasons we don't allow ourselves to reflect on our real feelings is because it's hard. It's painful. It takes courage to see your insecurities and your part in unhealthy dynamics. It's important for us to look at the real feelings behind blanket emotions such as anger to understand why we act the way we act and feel the way we feel.

It's time to go deeper. Stop taking things on a superficial level. Stop reacting in low self-esteem and start responding to others and yourself with loving kindness. You can begin moving toward being a better version of yourself by looking at the genuine, authentic feelings and insecurities you need to overcome.

Take a moment to review what you've accomplished in this chapter. You've learned how to identify the feelings beneath your anger. You've learned that others act as a mirror for your own feelings, and you've learned to identify the traits and qualities in others that you share, struggle with, and react to. Most importantly, you have the knowledge and understanding to develop actionable strategies to help you succeed.

Revisit this chapter — and especially your notes — from time to time. Review your notes about the challenges that you have identified in your life, and the goals that you set for yourself. Ask yourself how much closer to your goals you are today than when you began. Think about the next steps that will take you closer to your goal.

## EXERCISE

Identify, examine, and explore the real emotions beneath blanket emotions, such as anger, sadness, nervousness, and frustration. Commit to improving communication within yourself and with others. Commit to responding authentically and compassionately to others, rather than reacting to others in pain. Strive to go deeper into your emotions to understand your real feelings and how others reflect your feelings back to you.

Think of the people and situations that cause you to experience anger. Choose one person/situation that is troubling you. Explore the real emotions beneath your blanket emotion of anger.

In this situation — or with this person — imagine responding more authentically, with more compassion and understanding, rather than in anger. How would your responses be different?

_____

_____

_____

_____

_____

_____

_____

_____

_____

_____

_____

_____

_____

_____

_____

List other situations in which improving communication within yourself and with others would improve the outcome.

_____

_____

_____

_____

_____

_____

_____

_____

_____

_____

_____

_____

_____

_____

_____

_____

_____

_____

_____

_____

# CHAPTER 8
# MEDITATION

Many people are confused about what meditation is, what it means, and its benefits, never mind how to meditate. Most people don't realize that meditation isn't some foreign concept. We all do it from time to time, more often than we realize. We do it in little snippets here and there. We don't understand how meditation comes in. In this chapter, we'll explore meditation and facilitate building your confidence to commit to adding a daily practice with intent.

Mindfulness meditation is about you connecting to you. It's a connection to yourself. The balance in your life that you are seeking requires that you learn how to turn inward, rather than focusing on what is outside of you. You are the common denominator in your life, so why would you seek answers outside?

We wake up in the morning, jump out of bed, and spend much of our day in our head, helping others, taking care of things, fulfilling responsibilities, playing out roles at work, socializing, and affirming intimacy. We do most, if not all of it, with an external focus.

## BREAKING IT DOWN

I'm going to break down meditation so you begin to understand how you, in one form or another, meditate every day. Once you understand what meditation is and how it manifests in your daily life, you can set a goal of increasing the amount of time you go inward in your daily life, and begin to enjoy the benefits of spending a little less time 'in your head.'

When you are connected to the moment, to the absolute present time, you are meditating! Athletes call it being *in the zone*, photographers call it *the pocket*, those moments where you lose the concept of time and space. When you lose the concept of time and space, you are completely connected to the present moment. When you live in the present, in the moment, you simply experience, do and act. This is you, connecting to your senses with complete presence and focus.

Imagine those days when you're hanging out with your friends and check your watch and say: "Four hours went by. How did that happen?" This is when you are completely in the moment. When you're in the zone, you lose the concept of time and space and you feel great experiencing the moment with all your senses … fully present and just doing. You're in that bubble of energy where you're connected to all of your senses, and you are experiencing, doing, and acting in life. There is no worrying, ruminating on past experiences, or forecasting worst-case scenarios here! You are fully in the present, experiencing your authentic, true, amazing self.

## THIS IS MEDITATION

When you're in the moment, you're fine. You're perfect. This is meditation. You have gone inward and you are connecting to your perfection. You are yourself, and you're doing exactly what you want to do, fully present, experiencing your senses.

But here's where the problem comes in: sometimes we leave the moment and go into our heads and ruminate on the past or the future. The past is comprised of memories. We often go to negative memories and relive events that we're afraid of repeating.

Or our mind goes to the future. We know that the future is just our imagination … but instead of imagining what we want to manifest, we often imagine worst-case scenarios. We're afraid. We don't know if we can handle things so we start imagining things that could go wrong as a means of protecting ourselves by preventing or controlling various imagined situations. We start ruminating over dreaded 'what-if' scenarios. 'What ifs' are nothing more than worries. What if this happens? What if that happens? We start forecasting worst-case scenarios, catastrophizing, and bring in the doubting mind: imagining a future where things might go wrong because we want to be prepared for the worst that could happen. We spend so much precious time trying to prevent possible harm, to control life, that we forget to live.

## PAST AND FUTURE

The past and the future are just thoughts. Your thoughts are — plain and simple — your own judgments. Remember, life is just a series of experiences that we judge and label as positive or negative. We often generate negative future projections because we are afraid of repeating negative past experiences or mistakes. Fear is simply self-doubt. Doubting our ability to handle difficult situations, we sometimes choose to take ourselves to places in our imagination that we fear to prepare ourselves for the worst.

The truth is, we can't prepare ourselves. Even if you spend huge portions of your time trying to prepare for potential disasters in your life, if and when a disaster actually does happen, you'll deal with it in the moment by doing whatever feels appropriate. What comes out in the moment isn't often what we planned. But meanwhile, by thinking about it, you're just imagining something that could happen. Remember, what you focus on expands. By focusing on potential worst-case scenarios, we stay in a negative state. Why not, instead, consider best-case scenarios and promote a positive state of mind?

## POSSIBLE VERSUS PROBABLE

Anything is possible, but what is probable? Many times people with anxiety and depression overestimate the probability of bad things happening. Everything is possible in life, and yes, bad things can happen at times, but should we live each and every day constantly worrying about worst-case scenarios versus living our life imagining what we want to manifest?

## BACK TO MEDITATION

In the present, in the moment, you're completely connected, enjoying something with all your senses. For example, say I bake a loaf of banana bread. I smell it. I taste it. It's wonderful, it's perfect while I'm doing it, in the moment. But then I say, "Oh shoot, I think the last time I made this, it tasted better." Suddenly I am out of the moment; I have gone to the past and am critical. I compare the present negatively to an experience from the past, and I'm regretting the difference. Then, my mind jumps to the future. "Next time I make this recipe, I need to do this and that to it, which will make it better." Suddenly, I'm scrutinizing, judging, and criticizing my moment. I ruin the moment by getting into my head and comparing my past or forecasting my future actions. As a result, I miss the full experience of my wonderful, tasty banana bread in the here and now.

Many times, this is exactly what we are doing. We leave the moment, and we go into our heads and start to criticize, scrutinize, and judge, to compare or forecast worst-case scenarios.

**In the exercise at the end of this chapter, you'll have the opportunity to reflect on how much time you spend reliving your past mistakes and negative experiences, and forecasting worst-case scenarios.**

## PRACTICE THE PAUSE

To take control, we need to learn to practice the pause. Here's how. Start adding simple practices daily that take you into the moment. For example, I take a moment to go inward and feel grateful for the food I am eating. I take a moment to be thankful for it. Slow down to take that first bite of food. Really connect to the present moment of enjoying that first bite, rather than staying in your head and missing the experience of enjoying your food.

Do little things that give you joy and pleasure. These are the things that keep you in the moment. Activities, interests, and pursuits that you love are what allow you to lose the concept of time and space: hobbies, activities, interests, outings, moments of reflection where you're doing things that hold you in the zone, and where you're engaging in things fully present.

## S.T.O.P.

I'd like to introduce you to S.T.O.P., a simple method of introducing mindfulness into your daily life. You simply Stop, Take a breath, Observe yourself in the moment, doing one thing with complete presence. Then Proceed with your day.

Here's how it works.

**Stopping** takes us out of our heads from ruminating and self-critical talk.

**Taking a breath** keeps us in the moment and holds us there. It grounds and relaxes us a bit.

**Observing** yourself allows you to truly experience a moment in full presence and connection to yourself.

**Proceeding** takes you back to whatever you're busy doing but in a healthier state, more grounded and present. Try to proceed *in the moment,* to really feel things. Feel your fingers washing your hair, feel the toothbrush on your teeth and your gums when you're brushing your teeth. Taste the chocolate as it's melting in your mouth. Feel the kiss when you kiss someone. Feel the hug, the warmth, and the heartbeat when you hug someone. Learn to slow things down and connect with all your senses to experience the moment fully.

Right now, take a moment. How do your feet feel touching the floor, your fingertips touching the page? Your back on the chair, your posture, your breathing? As you breathe, feel the cool air coming in through your nostrils and the warm air leaving your body as you exhale. Feel your abdomen expand as you inhale and deflate as you let go of that breath.

Take the time to slow things down in your daily life. Observe them differently and realize that the more you bring yourself into the present the less you're in your head. As I said before, the past and the future are just thoughts, and thoughts are just self-made judgments.

In the next few chapters we will look at where some of those judgments come from — our parents, society, the pressures we put on ourselves — all our thoughts.

Anxiety and depression, by the way, are thought disorders — they only exist when you're in your head. When you are in the moment, you do not feel anxious or depressed. Notice that when you are free of anxiety, depression, and negative thoughts, you're often enjoying interests, hobbies, or the company of loved ones, with complete presence, engaged with your senses, rather than judging the experience.

When I work with patients, I try to bring them to a place where they practice the pause frequently throughout the day while enjoying hobbies, interests, or anything they enjoy, to allow themselves to be in a place where they are connecting to the moment and learning how to expand the practice of meditation.

Take the time to reflect on your life. Are you living in the moment every day, more and more, less and less, or not at all? Understand that meditation is nothing complex or mysterious; it's living in the moment with the complete presence of your senses. Give yourself permission to get in the zone and enjoy your life experiences without scrutiny, worry, and self-judgment. Connecting to the moment as many times as you can in a day is healthy. Then, as you master that, you can also notice the content in your head becoming more positive and happier. Gradually, when we *are* in our minds, we will find ourselves in a less threatening and anxiety-provoking place.

## EXERCISE

Think about the thoughts that run through your head on any given day. How much time do you spend reliving your past mistakes and negative experiences? How often do you forecast worst-case scenarios?

List your recurring and pervasive negative thoughts about the past and worst-case scenario outcomes.

_____

_____

_____

_____

_____

_____

_____

_____

_____

_____

_____

_____

_____

_____

_____

_____

_____

_____

_____

List the activities, interests, and pursuits that give you joy: the things in your life that allow you to lose all sense of time and live in the moment. Include things that you have yet to explore.

List strategies that would enable you to incorporate more meditative activities into your life.

_____

_____

_____

_____

_____

_____

_____

_____

_____

_____

List the obstacles that hold you back from meditating

_____

_____

_____

_____

_____

_____

_____

_____

# CHAPTER 9
# WORTHY OF LOVE

There's an ultimate need each and every one of us has in life: to feel worthy of love. I learned the worthy of love concept from the book, *Born on the Mountaintop*, by Freedom and Satyam Malhotra.

Merriam Webster defines love as: "a strong affection for another arising out of kinship or personal ties, an attraction based on sexual desire, affection based on admiration, benevolence, or common interests, an assurance of affection, and/or a warm attachment, enthusiasm, or devotion." In our extensive array of interpersonal relationships with the people in our life, every one of us strives to feel worthy of love. We place conditions on ourselves in order to be worthy of love, and in doing so we put a lot of pressure on ourselves. In fact, it's the first of many conditions we place on ourselves in life.

Our earliest experience of seeking validation of our worthiness — otherwise known as the external validating the internal — is seeking the approval of our parents. If Mom and Dad say "good girl" or "good boy," we feel that we are worthy of their time, attention, and affection.

As we proceed through life, we continue to seek validation and worthiness from other sources, and as we do, we often place tremendous conditions on ourselves and go to great lengths to feel worthy. For example, I have a first-generation Canadian patient from an Asian family. When he reached the point in his life where he was considering his career choices, I asked him what he wanted to be. He said: "I want to be an architect but I'm going to be a doctor."

I asked: "Why don't you do what you want and be an architect?"

He replied: "My parents are immigrants. They came here for me, and they want me to be a doctor. I can't disappoint them."

I asked: "If you disappoint your parents by becoming an architect, are they going to stop loving you?"

His response: "Of course not, but they'll be disappointed. And if they're disappointed, I'm going to be disappointed in me."

This young man's response implies that he's worthy of love only if his parents approve of his career choice. Not only that, if he follows his dream of becoming an architect, he is not worthy of his parents' love, and feels less than as a person, thus unworthy of self-love and self-respect because he has disappointed his parents.

## OUR FIRST CONDITION

This is the first condition in which we place ourselves: to feel worthy is to gain the approval of our parents. Then, we unwittingly become addicted to making our mother and father approve of our behaviors. What follows is a pattern of approval seeking.

## EXTERNAL VALIDATES INTERNAL

When our parents are happy with us, we are happy with ourselves. But this is only the beginning of the conditions we heap upon ourselves as we grow into adulthood.

As we move through our lives, the cycle continues and expands. I'm worthy of love if I get an education. If I don't get an education, I feel *less than*. I'm worthy of love if people like me. I'm worthy of love if I get that dream job, house, or car. I'm worthy of love if I do things perfectly and have good skills. I'm worthy of love if I marry the right person. I'm worthy of love if I dress well, look good, and am a good parent. I'm worthy of love if I live a moral life. And there are many more conditions we hold onto.

This chapter is all about being worthy of love. We'll examine the conditions we place on ourselves. These conditions can be endless and lead an individual to live an inauthentic life of pleasing others at their own expense.

## TERMS AND CONDITIONS

Let's take a look at some of the typical terms and conditions we place upon ourselves.

We can always do more people pleasing to make people like us. We can always do more approval seeking from our parents, friends, and associates. We can always seek higher levels of education or academic achievements. We can always find a better job, put more money in the bank, or aspire to have a better home. We can aspire to do things more perfectly. We can strive to become a better partner, a better parent, dress better, look better, and work smarter and harder. We can be more observant of our religion and live by a higher moral code. These conditions can become bottomless pits of expectation that we place on ourselves. The more you're trying to make everybody happy, the more certain it becomes that you will one day burn out trying to keep up with the cycle of doing things for the sake of others at your expense.

These are bottomless pits we can never fill. But we never stop trying! It fills a void temporarily but drains us over time. This can lead to feeling empty, drained, and unhappy. Over time, the lack of authenticity that comes from trying to please others or meet these many conditions can cause us to feel disconnected from ourselves and experience symptoms of anxiety and depression.

Here's the problem: in seeking validation and approval from others you sacrifice your own needs, desires, possibilities, and potential, often without realizing it. Mired in expectation and pleasing others, we often sacrifice our own authenticity and interests.

**In the exercise at the end of this chapter, you'll have the opportunity to explore the conditions and pressures you place upon yourself to please others.**

## THE CURE

Here's the antidote: you need to question whether you are doing or having something in order to be someone. Are your choices authentically your own, or are you doing what you feel others expect of you? The reality is that from the time you were born, you were worthy of love — just the way you were. In other words, you have always been and will always be worthy of love just as you are. Placing conditions is a learned behavior that doesn't serve your highest and best self.

Most of us grow up unaware of this. As a result, as we progress through our schooling and into adulthood, the conditions continue to mount.

## YOU ARE WORTHY OF LOVE

You are worthy of love if you get into the school and program of your choice, but if you don't, you're still worthy of love just the way you are. You are worthy of love if people like you, and if someone is angry with you, you're still worthy of love just the way you are.

You are worthy of love if you have the ideal job, house, money, but if you don't have money, or are in debt, you are still worthy of love just the way you are. You are worthy of love if you do things perfectly, and if you've made a mistake or two, you're still worthy of love, just the way you are.

You can say: "I'm worthy of love if I marry the perfect partner, and if I get divorced, I'm still worthy of love just the way I am. I'm worthy of love if I dress perfectly, and if I don't, I'm still worthy of love, just the way I am. I'm worthy of love if I'm a good parent, and if my child turns out to be a criminal or a drug addict, I'm still worthy of love just the way I am. I'm worthy of love if I go to church regularly and take part in community activities, and if I don't or can't, I'm still worthy of love just the way I am." Pure and simple, you are worthy of love just the way you are, with or without acquiring things. Your value comes from being, not doing.

## BOTTOMLESS PITS

These conditions are, without exception, bottomless pits. The more you try to make everybody happy at your own expense, the more certain it becomes that you will one day burn out trying to keep up with the cycle of pleasing others.

The key is to question your choices and actions. Ask yourself: *Am I placing conditions on myself — things I need to do or have or be in order to be someone, or am I authentically choosing this for my own fulfillment?* You are worthy of love if your parents approve of your behavior and choices, but you're also worthy of love if you disappoint them. You are worthy of love just the way you are.

You are worthy of love if you get into the school and program of your — or your parents' — choice. You're also worthy of love just the way you are, whether you do well academically or not. You're worthy of love if people like you, and just as worthy if they don't. Whether people are pleased or angry with you, you're worthy of love just the way you are.

I am worthy of love if I have the ideal job, house, money, or partner. If I don't, I am still worthy of love just the way I am. I'm worthy of love if I do things perfectly, and if I've made mistakes, I'm still worthy of love, just the way I am. I'm worthy of love if I'm in a successful marriage, but if I get divorced, I'm still worthy of love, just the way I am. I'm worthy of love if I dress well, but if I don't, I'm still worthy of love, just the way I am. I'm worthy of love if I'm a good parent. If my child turns out to be a criminal or drug addict, I'm still worthy of love, just the way I am. I'm worthy of love if I go to church and if not, I'm still worthy of love, just the way I am. You can have everything you want, but even if you don't, you are still worthy of love, just as you are.

## WORTHINESS, DRIVE, AND SELF-LOVE

The truth is that you are worthy of love just the way you are, with or without the conditions you and/or others impose on you.

Many of us are driven. We set aggressive goals and place stringent conditions on ourselves. We think that we are not good enough if we don't have certain material possessions, achieve certain professional or personal targets, or behave in certain ways. We do not unconditionally love ourselves. We place conditions on loving ourselves.

You may prefer to try to make the people in your life happier with you. You may prefer to do well in academics, choose an ambitious career, or strive for a better job. Preferring means that with or without it you are worthy of love and okay. Preferring is setting a goal. But with or without it working out, you won't crumble. You are worthy, just as you are.

## LOVE WITHOUT CONDITIONS

When I see parents in my clinical practice, I often ask them this question: "Is there anything your child could do that could make you love them less?" Most parents respond that they might be disappointed in their children from time to time, but the truth is that whether they go through a break-up, lose a job, or go to jail — no matter what — they will always love their children just the way they are.

As parents, we can unconditionally love our children, but we all struggle with unconditionally loving ourselves. We need to model unconditional love to ourselves rather than being hard on ourselves while unconditionally loving others.

## EXAMINE YOUR EXPECTED SELF

Being well-adjusted to a sick society is unhealthy. We all have a true self with whom we align. It's who we want to be and what we want in life. But we also have an expected self who is all about other people's expectations or beliefs about who we should be.

Just what is the expected self? The expected self is what people want and expect of us. Those people are your parents, society, your peers, your faith community, and what they expect may be based on what your socioeconomic status dictates, what your age and gender dictate, or what your culture dictates. Look at all those expectations placed on you. Bear in mind that being well-adjusted to a sick society means that you're sacrificing yourself by molding yourself into everything that people want from you — at your expense. If you're not living the life you want, not striving for what you want for yourself, then whose life are you living?

Challenge yourself to look at your life today. Are you becoming what everybody wants you to be at the cost of your authenticity? Or are you living your life authentically, being your true self without being everybody's everything, and sacrificing the VIP (very important person) you should be to yourself?

It's important to start looking at your life, and the cycles of conditions you place upon yourself. What conditions do you place on yourself to be worthy of your own self-love — worthy, valued, and good enough?

**In the exercise at the end of this chapter, you will be tasked with reflecting on your life over the past five years to identify the conditions you have placed upon yourself.**

## GET TO KNOW YOUR AUTHENTIC SELF

In recent memory, many successful, high-achieving, high-profile celebrities, such as Robin Williams, Kate Spade, and Anthony Bourdain, have tragically taken their own lives. Highly successful people who on a superficial level seem to have it all — fame, successful careers, wealth, friends, and loving families — can be disconnected from their authentic selves. A lack of authenticity leads many people to a dark and dangerous place in their lives, regardless of how much they are loved and admired, and how much they have and have achieved. They were not content, healthy, and aligned with self-love, acceptance, and self-care.

When we're doing everything to participate in the race to the top, or striving to please others and be everybody's everything, we drain and exhaust ourselves because we're not operating from a place of truth. Instead, our energies come from a place of trying to keep up with a version of ourselves that makes other people happy at our own expense, but has no authentic connection to our true selves.

The emptier and darker we feel, the more we feel hopeless, alone, and unfulfilled. We can become overwhelmed and overburdened by mounting commitments that do not fulfill or nurture us in any way. But when we choose to take on responsibilities and commitments because they are authentically part of our true selves, we can move forward to a place of our choosing.

## WAVE THE MAGIC WAND

In the exercise at the end of this chapter, you'll be instructed to revisit your work in Chapter 2, where you waved your magic wand and explored your ideal self. Now, you'll have a chance to go deeper and explore what you really want. The purpose of this exercise is to explore your authentic interests, goals, and desires. What do you truly want in life? This is a wish list, and an inventory of your authentic interests, passions, and dreams for your life, what you have aligned with and dedicated yourself to.

## MAKING CHANGE

Changing a lifetime of validation seeking is hard — but not impossible. The good news here is that you know three important things that you didn't know before: the conditions that you have placed upon yourself, the conditions that others have placed on you, and that you have the ability to live your life free of these conditions if you choose to do so.

When it comes to creating meaningful change, two major factors come into play: your faith in yourself and your ability to make a change, and your fear of the unknown, of possible failure, or lack of confidence in your ability to commit to change or to succeed beyond your wildest aspirations.

Remember to consider your current job, friends, family members, and community as you begin to integrate your authentic choices into your life. Make note of the people and resources at hand that can help you, such as friends, a supportive employer, mentors, and other resources in your community.

At the same time, it's important to think about the people and situations that could be saboteurs, such as non-supportive individuals who are threatened by change or are envious of you, overwhelming and conflicting work, family, and social obligations, lack of available resources, discouragement after small set-backs, self-sabotaging settings, situations, and individuals, old traumas, bad habits, and lack of peer support.

**COMMIT TO YOURSELF**

As you move into creating meaningful change in your life, keep in mind that change is a process with both challenges and rewards. Allow yourself time and patience to work toward your ideal life. As you move through the challenges that change presents along the way, know that there will be times when you will be afraid of what lies ahead as you move away from living up to conditions that no longer serve you. Remind yourself that faith in yourself will carry you through the tough moments. Remember: make your faith bigger than your fear. Fear is self-doubt, a no-no when you are aligned with being in higher self-esteem.

Return to this chapter and your notes from time to time. Revisit the goals and strategies that you laid out for yourself in your notes. And identify the next steps that will take you closer to your goals.

At the end of the day, remember, your worthiness is unwavering; it is not tied to your achievements, activities, acquisitions, or how much you please or disappoint others or yourself. You are worthy of love just the way you are. You are a human being, not a human doer. And you deserve to fill your life with interests and pursuits that fill you with joy, connection, and worthiness, just as you are.

## EXERCISE

We are worthy of love just as we are. Sounds good, but most of us do not live this way at all. Many of us place overwhelming conditions on loving ourselves. We set impossible standards. We need to meet these nearly impossible standards in order to feel good about ourselves.

What conditions do you place on yourself in order to feel 'worthy?' What standards do you need to meet to feel 'good enough?'

_____

_____

_____

_____

_____

_____

_____

_____

_____

List the conditions you carry within yourself to feel worthy of love.

_____

_____

_____

_____

_____

_____

_____

_____

_____

_____

_____

_____

_____

_____

_____

_____

_____

_____

_____

What (or whose) standards do you need to live up to in order to feel worthy? Work on correcting this! After all, your journey is an individual one of self-discovery. Live your life for yourself and your growth.

_____

_____

_____

_____

_____

_____

_____

_____

_____

Commit to yourself. Review your notes from Chapter 2, where you waved your magic wand and explored your ideal self. What does your authentic, ideal self really want out of life? List your authentic interests, goals, and desires. (Another way to think about this is to imagine what you would do if you won a lottery and were free of obstacles and limitations preventing you from being who you want to be.) Make a wish list, and an inventory of your authentic self, your interests, passions, and dreams for your life.

What you focus on expands! Once you envision it, allow yourself to manifest it.

_____

_____

_____

_____

# CHAPTER 10

# GUILT

In this chapter, we are going to explore what guilt is all about.

People often struggle with feelings related to guilt. We rarely sit with our guilt or attempt to deconstruct, explore, and understand its components. What is guilt really about? Why does it keep happening? We often find ourselves enmeshed in guilt and feeling distressed, overwhelmed, and angry.

Guilt is simply a sign that there is a conflict around what you want versus what someone else wants from you. When we want to do something and no one complains about it or has other ideas about what we should be doing, it's all good. No guilt! We do and live as we please, aligned with what we want, what makes us happy. From self-care and work, to play, pleasure, and enjoyment, we do what we want or need to do on any given day until someone comes along and requests something different from us.

Many of us struggle daily because others place expectations on our time, focus, and energies. Often, others want something very different from us than what we want to give. When there is a conflict with what we want versus what someone else wants from us, guilt arises. Guilt is a signal that there is a dilemma we must address. That dilemma gives rise to the question: "Do I please myself, or please those who place expectations on me to do something different?"

## FOLLOWING OUR TRUTH

Our goal in life should be to follow our truth. Why? Because following our truth always leads to a greater good. When you are a child, you don't experience guilt because you are looking for guidance and direction. You're looking for growth and are open to being led by adults. You're looking to parents, mentors, siblings, or friends to guide you.

For example, you might look to your parents to determine whether a stranger is safe or not, or what to wear to a party or to school because you are still learning and developing into your authentic self. You are learning and modeling the behaviors of others.

There comes a time when you are no longer looking for that guidance. You go inward, weigh your facts and perceptions, draw your own conclusions, and guide yourself. You want to form opinions on your own. This is natural; it's part of the process of maturation and individuation, the process of becoming your own person with a unique identity, with your own thoughts, opinions, and preferences.

## PLEASING OTHERS AT OUR OWN EXPENSE

Often, we struggle at this point in life. Though it is natural to want to form our own opinions and live our own lives, we begin to perceive the possibility of disappointing those who have guided us in our lives when our opinion is not in alignment with theirs. To make everything okay, we begin to sacrifice what we want, what we think, and what we do. In short, we feel guilty for disappointing the people we love, and choose to please others at our expense. The result is costly — we disappoint ourselves and sacrifice our self-care.

## SELF-CARE VERSUS SELF-HARM

When we give in to others at the cost of our own authenticity, we promote self-sacrifice and self-harm by taking a back seat in our own life. But not doing what makes us happy can often make us angry. Anger turned inward is depression, which causes tremendous harm. We often do not realize the detrimental effects of going against ourselves, sacrificing our self-care, self-truth, and self-love.

When instead of being true to ourselves we align with others' opinions or agendas, we block others from learning the lesson that we have evolved, grown, and have our own unique and separate agenda. There comes a time when our family members and friends need to realize that while at one time they were able to guide and direct our opinion, that time has passed, and we need to move forward and forge our own lives and work to achieve our own goals and growth.

## SERVING YOURSELF

When we are in a place of self-care and doing what we want, we enrich ourselves. Here's an example: I want to wear a new blue silk shirt to a family event. As long as no one opposes my plan, it's all good. I wear the blue shirt to the event, and I'm happy. No problem. However, I pick up my parents on the way to the event and I find that my mother has bought me a white shirt that she is determined I should wear, and kindly asks me to change.

This is where guilt shows up. What is the guilt about? In this example, it is, of course, easy to see that the guilt is a signal of the conflict between my desire to wear a blue shirt and my mother's desire that I wear the white shirt she so generously gifted to me.

If I refuse my mother's request and wear the blue shirt, all is well. I am making my own decisions and living in alignment with what I want for myself and how I want to present myself to the world. I am happy and feel confident and grounded. However, when my mother insists on me wearing the white shirt, she is putting expectations on me to change and abide by her preferences and choices.

## ENTER GUILT

Enter guilt, the signal of a conflict between what I want for myself and what someone else wants for me. Guilt is a conflict that needs to be confronted and respectfully resolved in truth. This conflict occurs not only with family and friends but with society at large: your boss, your colleagues, your partner, your children. Anyone could show up with expectations of you at any time. Guilt can arise when there is a discrepancy between what you want for yourself and what others would like you to do or be.

When a problem or dilemma arises between yourself and someone else, it does not automatically mean that you need to bend to their expectations, soften, and sacrifice yourself to their demands. If you are experiencing guilt, it's a sign that you have an opinion, preference, or agenda of your own, and something else you'd rather do. There are times when we look for guidance from others: bosses, siblings, friends, or parents. When we are looking for direction, we tend to go along with what others tell us. But there are also times when we are not. When we begin to mature and form our own opinions and lessen or end our dependence on the guidance and opinions of others, guilt can show up when we feel guilt for contradicting someone with a different viewpoint or preference.

As we mature, we develop a sense of independence, and we find fulfillment in making our own choices rather than looking for others to guide us. Independence is all about choices. We choose as best we can, to live our lives as we want, in authenticity and alignment with ourselves, for our highest good.

But many times, we remain stuck in patterns from our childhood, of caving in, people pleasing, seeking affirmation. But our purpose in life is not to please others at our expense. When we are younger, we please others, but not out of self-sacrifice. We do it from a place of innocence, lack of knowledge, and for survival. We're at a stage of development where we're not oppositional, and truly want to align with others. But as we mature, we grow into our own person, with preferences and opinions of our own. If we choose to please others at our own expense, we disappoint ourselves. This is where the harm occurs: disappointing ourselves reinforces self-harm, poor self-care, and low self-esteem.

**In the exercise at the end of this chapter, you'll explore your guilt, its sources, and how to stop the cycle and accept growth as organic and healthy, something to celebrate, not be embarrassed about.**

### IT'S NOT ABOUT THE SHIRT!

Back to our earlier example. If I wear the white shirt my mother wants me to wear, I am disappointing myself. But it's not about the shirt. It's about me, training myself that it is okay to disappoint myself, to feel unhappy within myself to please others and to make and keep others happy at my own expense. This will lead to emptiness, sadness, and feelings of void and dissatisfaction within myself.

There is a second negative outcome of this shirt scenario. When I give into my mother's request — or demand — to wear the white shirt, I am standing in the way of her learning a valuable life lesson — the lesson that I have matured to the point where I am no longer a child and no longer need her opinion to dress myself and feel presentable in public. I have grown from her teachings and guidance and can do it for myself, in authenticity. She can be proud that she has taught me so well.

When I resist giving in to her direction and wear what I choose, she learns the valuable lesson that I have matured, and no longer need her direction and intervention. She can begin to accept that I am no longer dependent on her and that I have matured and can take care of myself. Our relationship, in turn, is given a chance to change, evolve, and expand in new ways. I enable her to grow and be the mother of her evolved adult daughter. She deserves the opportunity to be proud of my growth and her teachings, which have led to my self-sufficiency.

When I say that I appreciate her gift but I am going to wear what I have chosen for the event, I stop enabling her to live in the past and enable her to move into the next phase of our relationship, where she respects me as an adult.

## PART OF THE PROBLEM

We need to realize that when we sacrifice ourselves, we are part of the problem! We prevent others from changing their impressions of and interactions with us as we grow and expand. We all stay stuck in old habits and patterns.

Once in a while, we can choose to sacrifice what we want for someone else, but when we do it, it should not come with hurt and harm. What do I mean by that? When we act, we should always look at our intention. When our intention comes from a place of truth, meaning a good place, a place that does not intend to cause hurt and harm to someone else, even while we might hurt others, we are being true to ourselves. This is growth-oriented and therefore okay.

Here's another example. You go on a blind date. At the end of the evening, rather than vaguely allude to making plans with a person you have no interest in just to avoid an awkward moment, you let that person know that you are not interested. You thank them for their time and wish them well.

You may have caused them discomfort or pain in a moment, but your intentions were not harmful and came from a place of truth. All good! Acting from a place of authenticity, you wanted to be clear and fair, and honest. You told this person the truth in the moment. You may have caused them momentary hurt and harm, but you've spared them greater hurt and harm in the long run, which would most definitely be the result if you were to be misleading and deceptive over time.

## HURT AND HARM

There are times, though, when we seek revenge and cause hurt and harm. For example, your partner breaks up with you, but you are able to persuade them to get back together with you even though you have no intention other than to break up with them and cause them the same degree of harm they inflicted on you. The energy and intention here do not come from a place of truth. It is vengeful and negative, self-centered, and egocentric.

A final example of actions and intentions that hurt and harm is game playing. Here's another relationship example. You break up with someone you have broken up with over and over because you have finally realized that you're just not a good fit. Later, one lonely evening, you text or call. You tell yourself you're just saying hello in a moment of weakness. They respond, and in no time, you're back in a dead-end relationship. You know it will never change. You both know that you're not compatible, that things will never really change. You're just playing games with each other. It feels like and is manipulation and deceit. You're not only lying to another person, you're lying to yourself. You're also holding yourself back from being with the right person by settling for someone who is just a comfort and habit.

## TRUE TO YOURSELF

It is important to look at our intentions when we interact with others. Are we being true to ourselves, and honest with others? If we intend to act with truth and not harm others, then we are not causing harm. We are living our truth.

We are born alone, and we die alone. Your journey is about you learning and striving to become a better, higher version of yourself, regardless of your upbringing, circumstances, and the experiences you have lived through. It is important to recognize the role of guilt in our interactions with others and to strive to be aligned with our higher, better self.

Guilt is alleviated only when we understand it. Remember, guilt is a signal that someone wants something different from you than what you want for yourself. It is important to connect with your feelings and your intentions when interacting with others. When what you choose to do about your guilt comes from a place of authenticity and truth, you are living your life on your own terms.

# EXERCISE

Guilt is a red flag emotion! It's a signal that appears in your body indicating an internal conflict at play. Guilt is triggered by a dissonance between what someone else wants or expects from you and what you want. Guilt is a useless emotion and serves neither the recipient nor the person making uncalled demands. Want to stop guilt in its tracks? The solution is simple: don't cave into it! Stop misinterpreting the signal of guilt and start doing what aligns you with your truth.

This exercise is designed to familiarize yourself with the sources of guilt in your life, and its impact on your wellbeing.

Let's look closely at the last time someone made you feel guilty.

Describe the guilt signal (where it came from, what the signaler wanted from you):

_____

_____

_____

_____

_____

_____

_____

_____

_____

_____

How was this request out of alignment with what you wanted?

For what did you feel guilty?

Who in your life are you enabling?

_____

_____

_____

_____

_____

_____

_____

_____

# CHAPTER 11
# SHARING THE BURDEN

In life, we often find ourselves feeling lonely. Loneliness is an interesting concept because, in different societies and cultures, this feeling of loneliness varies greatly. In large cities, many people feel independent throughout their lives. They do not rely on one another. They are private and insular, and often feel very much alone and lonely. By contrast, in tightly knit European and Asian cultures, and among those living in smaller cities, towns, and rural communities, there is a greater sense of community: closer family involvement, and extended family support in raising children, and when conflicts like divorce, job loss, and bereavement arise, there is a support system in place. There is a strong sense of community support, neighbors support each other, and there is more sharing of burdens and stressors.

The sharing of burdens is a concept that applies to the therapist-patient relationship. One reason why therapy works is that a comfort level is established where there is someone available with whom you can share your burdens by baring your soul and talking about things without a filter. You're able to share and have mirrored back what is really going on in your life … your inner struggles with symptoms, negative thoughts, fears, and doubts.

You're also learning. We do not often learn in isolation. We learn from others. We often do not know what to do in our lives and find ourselves struggling to understand what is right and wrong. When we are children, we don't know everything, but in interacting with other children we find out that other kids also don't know how to tell time, tie their shoes, or do well on multiple-choice exams, or that we're not the only ones who struggle with math or reading. By talking to other children, we contextualize and normalize our struggles. We gain perspective and the courage to carry on beyond the struggle. We realize the struggle is real but feel less alone with the understanding that our struggles are not unique but experienced by many others.

It's not all that different for adults. Sharing our struggles, or our burden, with others, whether monumental or small, allows us to normalize and better understand our challenges and our suffering, and presents us with opportunities for support and knowledge on how to cope, treat, or work through situations that feel challenging in the moment.

## WE ARE ALL CONNECTED

The truth is that we are interconnected and learning from one another. Some cultures promote competition in which we are driven to compare ourselves to others and constantly feel judged as lesser than, or better than, everyone we encounter. We get caught up in presenting ourselves in an inauthentic manner, faking it until we make it. We show no signs of self-doubt or weakness. We isolate ourselves from others in hope that people won't uncover our issues and doubts.

Here's the reality — there is no weakness. Life is a series of experiences. We're all learning. We're all growing. We are at once perfect and a work in progress. And we're all trying to become better, higher versions of ourselves. What's more, we are interconnected and living a human life complete with difficulties, obstacles, and struggles while sharing joy, acceptance, love, support, success, and growth.

We are not meant to be perfect. Neither are others. We need to have compassion and empathy for ourselves as we grow and learn. We do the best we can with what we have, and we make the best decisions and choices we can with the knowledge and resources we have at our disposal.

What we know today is different from what we will know tomorrow. When I'm in Grade 3, I do the best I can with what I know, and when I am in Grade 5, I do the best I can with what I know. When I am in Grade 5, it would be foolish and harmful to look back at my Grade 3 self and punish myself for the immature behaviors and choices of my youth. In third grade, I had only Grade 3 life experiences and information. The two years in between have taught me so much that now, in fifth grade, I know better. Comparing is unfair and irrational.

## SCRUTINIZING, JUDGING, ADMONISHING

As adults, we do this to ourselves all the time. We scrutinize, judge, and admonish ourselves for the decisions we've made as though we could or should have made better, different decisions. The truth is that we do the best we can with what we know. We don't want to cause ourselves harm. At times, in ignorance or lack of knowledge or information, we do. We make decisions that do not serve our best interests. But we do not harm ourselves on purpose. We make suboptimal choices at times because we do not know any better.

For example, I am buying my first brand new car, and I have narrowed it down to two choices, car A and car B. I weigh my options, and doing the best I can with what I have and know. I end up purchasing car A. In time, I begin doubting my choice, and start to lose confidence in my knowledge of cars in general. I beat myself up about a decision I made in the past by wondering if car B was a better choice.

Here's the reality. After driving car A for a year, I can see its flaws. I have essentially expanded my knowledge set and now better see and understand what I like and dislike about this car. The reality is, I've learned a lot about cars.

But suppose I am right. Car A turns out to be a complete lemon, and car B ends up being the car of the year. The next time I purchase a car, I'll be a little wiser in making my decisions with my newly acquired information and won't make the same mistake again. Trust that in a moment we decide, we are choosing the best for ourselves with what we know at that time.

## LESSONS ALONG THE WAY

Life is just a series of experiences. We learn our lessons along the way. With these lessons, we expand our knowledge set. And each and every day, as we grow from childhood onward, we are expanding our knowledge set. We do the best with what we have in the present. You began reading this chapter with one knowledge set, and by the end of this chapter, you will have enhanced your knowledge. You've expanded. You've learned. You will never be who you were before you started reading this book. You will have grown and learned, and will be working on implementing your learnings in your life.

We tend to be hard on ourselves, to expect that we should know everything up front. And we beat ourselves up if we fall short. Again, life is a series of experiences that shape us and help us grow.

Along the way, we are surrounded by others who are having their own series of experiences and lessons. To live is to learn. This is what connects us to others. By holding back and not sharing our experiences with others, we hold ourselves back from opportunities to feel connected and to normalize our doubts, challenges, and struggles.

When other people share their struggles with us, we learn from their trials and errors as well, much to our own benefit. Alone, we are exhausted. But we can heal our tiredness through connection and rest.

## SELF-HELP AND WELLNESS

What are self-help and wellness really about? They're about you uncovering and discovering other aspects of yourself. It's you seeking knowledge and untapped resources. But it's also about you being honest with yourself and others.

In Chapter 1, we talked about the table with three legs. The legs represent our physical symptoms, negative thoughts, and lifestyles/behaviors. On any given day, all three of these elements are at play, intermingled and mushed up inside. We can become overwhelmed with physical symptoms and negative thoughts. Unhealthy behaviors or habits then emerge.

## SOFTEN AND RELAX

You don't have to be alone in all you carry. When we share our burden by connecting with others, we can sort out our physical symptoms and negative thoughts and behaviors, and begin taking steps to change. Self-help and wellness are about awareness. A key step in awareness is understanding ourselves. Other people could have more or different knowledge about what we are experiencing, and could help us by contributing to our knowledge set, just as we could contribute to theirs. There is strength in sharing. Explore new ways of being, learning, and growing.

## CONNECTING WITH OTHERS AND OURSELVES

Sharing our burden is also about slowing down … slowing down to connect with people and with yourself. In fact, to genuinely connect with others, you must first connect with yourself. Pause and reflect. Rituals are a great means of connecting to ourselves. A simple ritual, such as lighting a candle and sitting in silence for a few minutes, helps us slow down. Rest is what I call practicing the pause and connecting with how we are feeling. Keeping a gratitude log, taking a moment at the end of each day to reflect and record what you are grateful for, is another simple and powerful ritual.

We are all tired, exhausted on a variety of fronts. Let's unite, share, connect, and empower ourselves and others to heal. Foster healthy practices, habits, and interactions.

We can share our struggles, victories, and gratitude with others. And they can share theirs with us. From others, we can learn many things, including what we may be taking for granted. Through sharing our burden, we expand our knowledge set and deepen our gratitude. Sharing sorrow halves it; sharing joy doubles it.

If we don't connect with others, we limit our experiences, intellect, understanding, connectedness, and growth. We are here to live and love fully, not just go through the motions. Sharing our burden with others is crucial to our goal to stop existing and start living.

Live until you die. Don't just exist, life is too special for that. Live fully! Start now with yourself and with others. Sharing your burden is a part of the human journey. We are all in this together.

## EXERCISE

---

Reflect on the thoughts and beliefs that hold you back from connecting with others, sharing, and asking for help. Make note of how you could shift to connect authentically.

---

---

---

---

---

_____

_____

_____

_____

_____

_____

_____

_____

_____

What behaviors can you bring in to share deeper parts of yourself, be real with others, share pains and sorrows, and celebrate joys, gratitude, and love?

_____

_____

_____

_____

_____

_____

_____

_____

Sometimes we feel bad sharing our good qualities, gains, and successes because we don't want to appear arrogant. If you intend to be proud of yourself, don't hold back on being your own greatest fan. Celebrate you!

You don't need people to validate you. See the good in you and appreciate your own good skillset. Don't share to belittle someone or to show them you are better, as those intentions come from an unhealthy place of negativity. Instead, practice healthy self-praise and self-love to acknowledge your own good. It is acceptable to speak positively.

# CHAPTER 12
# FORGIVENESS

We all struggle with forgiveness because we do not fully understand it. Forgiveness is not something we do for others. It's about us processing our pain and understanding the hurts that we internalize resulting from experiences that we have judged as negative.

Life is, you will remember, just a series of experiences that we judge through our filters. We judge these experiences as positive or negative. I have learned through my own life that most people do not intend to cause us pain. But people in pain spill their pain onto others.

At times we encounter people who are acting out their negative, hurtful behaviors, abuses, and low self-value. They may be lying, cheating, withholding information, taking us for granted, being selfish, or punishing … the list goes on. Some of this is modeled behavior (behavior we learn from observing others), some is related to upbringing and values that they have learned within their family structures, and life experiences.

We may also feel hurt by others for our own reasons. If we have been tormented or abused, we may have ongoing trust issues. We may be inordinately hard on others because we learned to be hard on ourselves.

## VARIABLES AT PLAY

Often, when we are going through hurtful experiences, our pain is not as clear-cut as we think it is. There are many variables at play when it comes to others causing us pain. Other people, you will remember from earlier in this book, are mirrors that reflect ourselves to us in many ways.

We need to learn to take accountability when others cause us pain, and when we perceive and judge others as the cause of our pain, happiness, or healing. By this, I mean that we need to learn how to look at ourselves in our many contexts and settings with clarity and compassion. For example, I know myself as a daughter in front of my mother, a friend among my friends, a sister in front of my brother, an aunt with my nieces, a student in front of my teachers, and a therapist in front of my patients. Everything and everyone outside of myself is constantly revealing sides of myself to me — my likes, my dislikes, my strengths, my ego, and my challenges. A math exam might show me my shortcomings in that area, or an English exam might reveal how much calmer and collected I am in that milieu.

## TALK ABOUT FORGIVENESS

Everyone and everything we interact with reveals something about ourselves to us. Often, when we talk about forgiveness, it's about people. We get hurt, and our hurts are, for the most part, people-related. When I say there is a mirror between ourselves and others, I mean that we are judging them through our own filters. Your issues from growing up, your schemas, or the maps in your head about how things need to or should be ... it's all at play.

When someone aligns with the way we feel things need to be, we feel a level of comfort. We feel comfortable with them and may even feel comfortable enough to like them. When someone doesn't match up to our version of the way things should be, we often feel uncomfortable or distrustful. We may not like them or trust them. We might judge them negatively or reject them completely.

## EXPLORING OUR PATTERNS

Sometimes we need to take a step back from our initial impressions and reactions and explore what our feelings are really about. We've all heard the term *chemistry*. Chemistry has nothing to do with chemistry — it's all about familiarity. Though you may not recognize it in the moment, the person with whom you feel an instant connection may be just like your father, sister, mother, mentor, brother, or friend.

We often repeat patterns but fail to recognize those patterns until later in the game. There is a mirror in each and every person that comes to you. If, for example, I walk by you wearing the same scent your Aunt Matilda used to wear, you may instantly like or dislike me (depending on how you feel about Aunt Matilda). If Aunt Matilda used to whack you with a stick, you just might hate me by association. If she was sweet and kind and used to bake your favorite cookies and take you to the park to play, you might have an instant like for me without my earning such a bond with you. You might judge me as kind and caring without knowing a single thing about me.

We make a lot of judgments without knowing why, or how. What's this got to do with forgiveness? Good question!

We go through a lot of pain and hurt caused by other people. But most people do not intentionally cause others harm. They behave the way they behave as a consequence of their experiences and upbringing. We often have conflicting ideas about what is right and wrong. We often do not relate to the way others see the world, and we cause each other pain, sometimes out of ignorance, other times out of our own fears and insecurities.

When we are children, we are in a place of high self-esteem. We are also in a place of innocence and ignorance. We believe in the good. But as we grow and experience hurts, they strip us of our innocence. We learn that others can hurt us and that we can fall down and hurt ourselves. We learn through experiencing pain that our safe, happy, and secure picture of the world might not be an accurate one.

Likewise, with people we start out on a positive front, trusting and hopeful, and through ongoing experiences, we begin to see different sides of one another. These experiences can cause us conflict, pain, disagreements, disappointments, and hurts.

## LOOK DEEP INTO THE MIRROR

It is important to look deeply into the mirror and see what the mirror is showing and teaching you, not only about the other person but about yourself. Learned beliefs about yourself that are not necessarily true, with reinforcement, can feel true.

For example, if I were dating someone for five years and it was an abusive relationship, I would not only need to forgive them for the hurt they caused, I would also need to forgive myself. I would have to forgive my partner for causing me harm and would have to forgive myself for putting up with it longer than necessary. I would have to forgive myself for loving the other person more than I loved myself. I would have to forgive myself for believing that this person would change when they had been consistently causing me harm. I have to forgive myself for not loving myself enough to walk away from something hurtful and harmful. I have to forgive myself for putting their needs ahead of my own. I have to forgive myself for not seeing the truth. And I have to forgive myself for staying in a situation that lowered my sense of self-worth and self-esteem.

## THE GAMES WE PLAY WITH OURSELVES

We have to be accountable to ourselves for those times when we put blinders on and refuse to see the red flags or acknowledge the truth about situations that are hurtful, painful, risky, harmful, or dangerous. We have to acknowledge our part in remaining in relationships and situations that lower our self-esteem out of fear that we will never meet anyone better.

We need to look at the games we play with ourselves so that when we forgive those who cause us pain, we can also understand our own part in the story. Why did this person come into my life? What are they showing me about my own lack of self-esteem? Are they showing me that I love others at great expense to myself? They are showing me that I put up with abuse.

Even when someone has done you harm, the story in its entirety is unlikely to be solely a painful one. Usually, when a person enters into your life, it is on a positive note. It is near the end that we focus on the bad. But this person may have brought you good, or at least good in the form of the growth of a skillset to handle the bad they brought in.

**In the exercise at the end of this chapter, you'll be asked to choose a person with whom you've had a negative personal relationship, or a business partnership that has gone sour, or a boss that is hard on you, and you will be guided through the process of writing a forgiveness letter. In this letter, you will be taking the important step of acknowledging the entire story of a relationship, the good, the bad, the hurt and harm, accountability for your part, the growth, lessons, and steps forward that resulted from this person entering into your life story.**

We need to recognize that all suffering, hurts, pains, and sorrows are catalysts for change. Forgiving those who have hurt us means that we are letting go of the personalization of a negative experience and allowing ourselves to move forward by understanding its lessons. Getting caught up solely in the pains and negatives can lead to our own demise.

You need to see the various parts, within a shared story, take accountability, and realize that in every situation of pain, there's learning and growth. Through life-changing traumatic events, we often personalize the impacts and see ourselves as *less than*. But such experiences teach us self-compassion, love, rest, and healing. Our traumas — like all of our life experiences — teach us. You have a choice to release yourself from your pain through forgiveness, rather than personalizing it and carrying it as a weight in fear of it repeating. Keep that in mind as you work on this exercise.

## EXERCISE

Think of someone from your past with whom you've had a negative relationship — personal, business, or someone in your family.

On a separate piece of paper, using the instructions below, write this person a letter of forgiveness. In this letter, you will be taking the important step of acknowledging the entire story of this relationship and forgiving this person.

This letter is a form of therapeutic processing. It is for you, but if you feel in your truth you want to share it with the person, you may choose to do so. But before sharing ask yourself: What is the purpose of sharing this letter? If this person is out of your life, and you feel this is a healthy boundary, you may not want to disrupt the status quo. Remember, this forgiveness letter is principally for you and no one else.

• **Begin with the story of how you came to be involved with this person.** If, for example, this person is a former boss, begin with what inspired you to want to work for them, for example, how you saw them as a brilliant, inspiring leader and a valuable mentor.

• **Then outline the hurt and harm that came to you.** What hurt you, made you insecure, doubtful, eroded your confidence, or caused you pain and suffering? Tell the whole story of what went wrong, how you may have disappointed them, and how they failed to live up to your idealized version of them. Outline the times you felt judged, criticized, passed over, disrespected, less than in comparison to others, and so on.

• **Next, go deeper into the reasons this person entered into your life.** What did this person teach you? Maybe they showed you how easily you lost faith and belief in yourself, how you were quick to doubt and judge yourself negatively in front of your competition. Maybe they taught you that overcompensating in the face of competition alienates others from you and makes them turn away from you. Perhaps seeing others receive compliments and praise revealed to you a lack of openness, ability, or willingness to collaborate with others at your own level. Perhaps the boss reflected insecurities, jealousy, envy, laziness, etc. Share the insights and lessons you carry with you as a result of your hurtful experiences.

• **Now review your part in the situation.** What could you have done differently? How could you have reacted and interacted more positively in the situation? What did you learn, and how have you grown as a result of your experiences with this person?

• **Finish with a statement that provides you with closure.** You are now ready to conclude the letter with a statement of closure. This statement acknowledges that while this person has caused you pain, this experience has also taught you to become a better, higher version of yourself.

You now choose to focus on your strength and self-growth, rather than the story of pain from this encounter.

List all that you have learned and the lessons that have moved you forward. End with the statement that you choose to let go of the hurts, criticisms, and other negative experiences, and take away from the interaction the lessons of growth. Thank them for entering your life and for teaching you valuable lessons, perhaps about your own self-esteem, about how much you value other people's opinions of you over your own. In closing, clear the negativity and hurts from your interactions by forgiving them for all intentional and unintentional hurts, and forgive yourself for being so hard on yourself and personalizing the experience. Acknowledge the experience for the lessons it taught you and the growth and betterment it made possible.

Here's a sample closing statement:

"Thank you for teaching me and helping me grow. I appreciate your lessons and release all hurts I carry within. I set myself free of [list] and I choose to close this exercise through this simple ritual, or act." (Create a simple ritual for yourself to symbolize closure. For example, you could burn, tear up, or store this letter somewhere safe and secure as an act of closure.)

Use the space below to explore your thoughts about forgiveness, who you wish to forgive, and how forgiving someone makes you feel.

_____
_____
_____
_____
_____
_____
_____
_____
_____
_____
_____
_____
_____
_____
_____
_____
_____
_____

# CHAPTER 13
# GRATITUDE

More often than not, we tend to focus on what we are missing in life. Rather than see the glass as half full we are constantly looking at what we lack. We need to look at life accurately. Gratitude is a way to do just that — to look at life clearly and with accuracy.

One of the reasons that we focus on the negative is that there is a part of each and every one of us that is afraid of getting hurt, afraid of repeating our patterns of pain and suffering. We hold onto our pain so that it doesn't repeat itself, and what ends up happening is that exactly what we are resisting shows up over and over again in different forms.

Whatever we resist, so the saying goes, persists. For example, if I say to you: "Don't think about a pink monkey with a purple banana," your mind automatically goes there. Even though I asked you not to think of a particular image, your mind goes there because what you resist persists.

It is important for us to become more aware of the habit of focusing on the negative and learn to shift to a more positive focus on our past, live in the present, and manifest a positive future.

## IN THE MOMENT

In Chapter 8, we explored meditation, the practice of living in the moment. When we are living in the moment, the present, we simply experience, do, and act. We are connected to our senses.

When we leave the present, our minds go to the past or the future. When we go to the past, we look at memories, more often than not negative memories, since we don't want them to repeat. We replay regrets, we compare our present situation to our past, we scrutinize, we judge. Or our minds go to the future, and when we go to the future what do we do? That's right — we forecast negative scenarios out of fear or self-doubt, we worry about repeating past mistakes, we imagine reliving past hurts, or, worse, having a worst-case scenario come to life.

The future is just our imagination. But rather than planting the seeds of what we would like to happen, we envision what we are afraid of. We want so badly to avoid negative situations, yet we catastrophize and imagine the worst. Our past and our future are nothing more than our thoughts and judgments about life. Anxiety and depression are thought disorders. They exist only when we are in our heads, thinking about the negative aspects of our past and projecting negativity into our future.

Here's the good news, and the crux of the lesson of this chapter: we can take charge of what we think about. We can refocus our thoughts on the positive memories from our past, and rather than planting the seeds of worst-case scenarios for the future, we can instead plant the seeds of best-case scenarios, of things that we want to manifest and bring forth.

People often say to me, "this is hard." But it only feels hard because you have reinforced negatives for so long. Remember, you were born innocent and positive; you acquired the negative as you grew. Time to unlearn and get comfortable with the positives with which you've lost touch.

Most of the time, though we may not realize it, we spend most of our day, consciously and unconsciously, in self-scrutiny, in negative evaluation, and in negative judgment. But we have the power to choose to focus on the positive rather than the negative.

### BREAKING AN OLD HABIT

Gratitude is a very simple and powerful way of breaking this habit. In our meditation chapter, we explored the value of establishing rituals as a way of practicing the pause. Here it is back again. But this time, we're going to get even more specific and explore practicing the pause for positivity. Instill in a pause an uplifting mantra, an affirmation, a reframing statement or self-praise, and gratitude.

### WELLS AND BRIDGES

The truth is, as much as we suffer in our life — remember that suffering is a catalyst for change to take you to a better place — suffering contains many aspects of wells and bridges, beautiful moments of positivity, opportunity, and shifts with supports. You may not be acknowledging such things, but they are present.

Let's use wells and bridges as a metaphor for exploring this powerful catalyst for change. Wells represent the many opportunities for abundance and growth that have manifested throughout your life unexpectedly. Bridges represent the opportunities and situations that have shown up to help you through times of trouble. When you examine your life story through this metaphor, you will discover that you have been blessed with many wells and bridges in your life.

Think about friends who have come to your aid when you needed help, the teacher who noticed that you were sad or not yourself in school, the mentor who showed up at a time when you needed inspiration. These bridges carry you over troubled times and waters.

Look at the many times in your life when you have been sent blessings in the form of wells or bridges, through friends, mentors, family members, and even strangers who share and disclose parts of their life experiences that relate to your own struggles and challenges. There are many bridges to keep you from becoming discouraged about your life and your sufferings, and to help you realize that you are being given exactly what you need to take you to the next level.

For examples of wells, recount jobs you obtained without preparation, people you magically connected with through networking or love, a winning lottery, a pregnancy after years of trying, a new job, a promotion, a passing grade when you thought you failed, recovery from an illness, surviving a serious car accident, etc.

**In the exercise at the end of this chapter, you'll have the opportunity to explore your wells and bridges.**

We need to make our faith bigger than our fear. We need to believe, not only in ourselves, but that everything has its place in our growth. We need to move beyond getting caught up in the negatives and focus on planting seeds of positivity. We need to acknowledge that despite what is lacking in life, there is much that is positive and beautiful, and much to be grateful for amongst the chaos and the challenging moments.

When you can see the many blessings in your life, despite any negativity in your past, and see the good amongst the bad, you have arrived at a place where you can transform from living in low self-esteem into high self-esteem, that is to say, the most authentic, highest and best version of you.

What goes around, comes around. Negative multiplies into more negative. It cycles downward, feeding off its harmful energy. If you call me stupid, I might react in kind, and our interactions could devolve into violence. But if you call me stupid and I am in touch with the good things in my life, I won't engage in the negativity and it will end there. I will give you a hug or in some other way break the cycle by not responding in the same energy, frequency, or vibration.

**BREAKING NEGATIVE CYCLES**

Remember, when people are in pain, their pain spills over onto others. We need to reflect on our truth, their truth, and the ultimate truth. We judge what is right and wrong from our viewpoint, and in turn, are judged by others from theirs. The goal is to live in your truth, own who you are and where you are at, at any given moment in time.

For example: Say I have a friend who is upset that she is always the one who makes plans and that I never take initiative. She is, of course, allowed to feel that way, given her blueprint and perspective. She may also have issues around people not reaching out to her. However, she has the time and energy to make social plans. And if she had compassion rather than judgment, she would see that I am so busy that I don't have time to make plans and that I appreciate her efforts and rely on her to do it.

From her perspective, she feels unappreciated, and that I am taking advantage of her. However, I am just really busy, and appreciate that my friend with the time and energy to make plans makes it easier for me, in my current work situation, my truth, and my life. If she is a true friend, she will let me know that, once in a while, she needs her friends to reach out, make an effort to make plans. Here, she brings awareness about something that bothers her, and supports change by letting me know she is upset and needs me to do something to fill her needs and her truth. And she has provided me with an opportunity to enrich our relationship by showing her that I respect her efforts and care about her feelings. But if she doesn't communicate with me, and stays upset, and puts her foot down, she has already made a judgment about me, which does not give me a chance to respond and change.

Many times, people judge you. There is simply no use in trying to convince them otherwise as they've already made up their minds about who you are. This is where you need to stand in your truth and say, "Not my circus … not my monkey." Own yourself and your truth, that your intentions are good and that a true friend would express their feelings and allow you to explain yourself and change, versus judging you and staying angry. Remember, when people are in pain, they spill onto others. We have a choice. We can take it on, or say, "thanks but no thanks; these are your feelings to own." I am not saying we do not get hurt or upset by peoples' actions. However, good health is indicated by our ability to bounce back from negative upset feelings. Explore how long you are stuck in conflicts, hurts, disappointments, upset feelings. Our ability to bounce back quicker by revising thoughts, reconceptualizing and letting go of past hurts to be in the moment is the goal for us all. If I've made someone upset unintentionally, that person should make me aware of their feelings. Because we all have our own unique blueprints, we may not be aware of what will be hurtful to another. You can demonstrate compassion. People want love. If they're causing you pain, before judging them, let them know, and give them an opportunity to change. Likewise, if someone doesn't allow you to change, and instead allows their pain to spill over onto you, you can choose to walk away.

You can choose to surround yourself with positive people with good intentions. Always take charge of the energy in your space. When you remove judgmental people from your life, you're making room for people who are more aligned with where you are today. Don't feel bad when people leave your life, cut you out, or block you on social media. Realize and accept that some relationships may be ending. Make room for healthier relationships that align with who you are today.

You can transform rather than engage in negative energy. If you can break cycles of negativity and refrain from throwing fuel on the fire by engaging in conflicts that make everything worse, you can bring yourself to a place where there is more positivity, calmness, control, ease, and happiness coming into your life.

**In the exercise at the end of this chapter, you'll be challenged to explore areas of negativity in your life, and how you might act to shift to a more positive state.**

Are you able to take hold of your moments and break cycles of negativity by being proactive and bringing in more positivity? You may not be at your best possible weight and figure, but are you able to recognize the beauty amongst the areas you are striving to improve? Are you able to recognize that you are not living in a worst-case scenario?

In many ways, gratitude is an exercise that involves you slowing down your day in order to give thanks for what is good in your life, what is going well today and in your life in general.

## TAKE A MOMENT

Take a moment of gratitude right now: for your feet that carry you where you want to go throughout the day and for your mind that enables you to think and work through things. Have a moment of gratitude for the people in your life who support you and love you, for the food that nourishes you and gives you the energy that carries you through a full day of activities. Be grateful for the moments that bring blessings, smiles, and love into your life.

Gratitude also combats negative thoughts and moods. Negativity is anger. Anger turned inward is depression. Anxiety is about self-doubt. We have cognitive distortions and worries ruminating in our minds during stress. Stay grateful. Practice the pause throughout the day. When we practice gratitude, we are strengthening our positivity, calming ourselves, and learning to focus on the good amongst the bad. As you focus on and are grateful for the good amongst the bad, you alleviate negative moods and symptoms of anxiety. Negative emotions and thoughts, as well as pessimistic ways of seeing the world, cannot persist where there is gratitude.

With gratitude, we replace darkness with light. Through positive affirmations, we plant seeds for hope for the future rather than forecasting worst-case scenarios. By having gratitude for the things that are working, we can lift ourselves out of negativity and depression, of loneliness, of feeling lost and alone without a sense of belonging in the world. Often, our negative thoughts are not accurate or true, yet we give them a lot of weight. Starting today, take a moment to bring gratitude into your life. Take five minutes every day to reflect on your day. Find gratitude in the little things that have sustained you. Be grateful for all the little things that made your day beautiful among the moments of stress, criticism, frustration, fatigue, illness, and responsibilities.

## EXERCISE

In this chapter, we learned that gratitude provides us with a way to look at our life clearly and that practicing the pause of gratitude empowers us to replace negative thoughts with positive ones. More importantly, when we practice gratitude, we shift from living in a state of lack and low self-esteem to a more positive state of high self-esteem. In the exercise below, we focus on creating a more positive perspective on our past, our present, and our future.

## PART ONE: WELLS & BRIDGES

Wells represent the many opportunities for abundance and growth in our lives. List your wells, including career, educational, social, and other opportunities that have enriched your life:

---

---

---

---

---

Bridges represent those who have shown up to help and guide you through times of trouble and pain. List the people in your life who have come to your aid in times of trouble:

_____

_____

_____

_____

_____

_____

_____

_____

_____

_____

_____

_____

_____

_____

_____

_____

_____

_____

## PART TWO: PRACTICING THE PAUSE FOR GRATITUDE

It takes just a few moments a day to stop and be thankful for the many good people, experiences, and comforts of your day. Take just five minutes and list the many features of your day for which you are grateful. Think about the people who support you, the food you enjoy, the clean air you breathe, your comfortable shoes, and your warm, comfortable bed.

_____

_____

_____

_____

_____

_____

_____

_____

_____

_____

_____

_____

_____

Moving forward…

Make this five-minute gratitude pause a daily ritual, and if and when you're having a bad day or thinking negative thoughts, revisit this exercise and lesson to renew your commitment to an attitude of gratitude, and shift from a negative mindset to a state of high self-esteem.

# CHAPTER 14
# SELF-WORTH

Let's talk about self-worth and self-esteem. Self-esteem is really about loving yourself as you are, which is a hard thing to do. Why is it so hard? This is a very good question.

We are born in high self-esteem. We are born in a place of purity and innocence, living in the moment, unconditionally loving, the very definition of high self-esteem. Children show us this when they welcome everyone with love. They smile and laugh and hug and kiss everyone, even those who don't return their affections. Children act as if they're all-powerful and capable of anything. They're going to be astronauts, firefighters, doctors, scientists, teachers, bus drivers, construction workers, artists … anything and everything they see that excites them. They see only good and play, fun, love, and smiles. Six-year-olds laugh on average 300 times a day, and adults, 50-100 times daily.

Children speak with confidence, from a place of truth and strength. They look in the mirror and see and accept themselves as they are. You don't hear children saying: "I'm too fat," "I'm unworthy," or "I need to lose 10 lbs." They see only their own beauty. And they are engrossed in living in the moment, playing, and loving happily.

They live in the moment — the here and now — because that's all they know. Summers seem endless. That months-away promised trip to Disney World means nothing other than their joy in the moment it is mentioned to them.

Children walk around in high self-esteem. Their innocence is their strength. They speak from a place of truth, often blurting out embarrassing comments about people and situations they see.

Along the way, the adults in their lives teach them to check themselves, question their truth, and proceed with caution. "You can't walk around naked. Put on some clothes!" We erode their high self-esteem by teaching them to question what feels good and natural to them.

Living in their superhero truth, speaking out, being playful, having no fear as they move into the world, we temper their behaviors and they learn that there are limitations to their abilities. We warn them that they have much to learn about living in the world.

On the inside, they are purity, love, and excitement for living in the moment, and their self-esteem exudes love unconditionally, without judgment or scrutiny. We teach them to hold back their truth and fit in and be socially appropriate.

As children grow, they begin to question themselves. Are they really that superhero with high self-esteem? Or are they the roles they play: the good little girl who listens in school rather than laughing and playing with her friends, the well-behaved young boy who sits still on the school bus when he feels like running up and down the aisle screaming at the top of his lungs?

## THE ROLES WE PLAY

Let's look at the roles we play in our lives. First, we're children, grandchildren, perhaps siblings, we're students, friends, parents, professionals, and partners. On the inside, we may still harbor that superhero. On the outside, as we grow, we take on many roles in the course of our lives.

These roles we play are in large part a product of our environment, and the modeled behaviors and activities we see. *Monkey see; monkey do.* The way my mother fries eggs is the way I will do it because I learned it from her. We learn how to play the roles we take on from the people around us. We can shift, but that takes conscious awareness and practice.

If you are a child with high self-esteem who lives with a parent who calls you "stupid" for years, what happens? After several years, you begin to believe this to be true. You start to fear that this could be true. Maybe your parent is right, and you are stupid. Over time, you arrive at a place of low courage where you no longer challenge your parent's negative statement. You have internalized their assessment and made it official — you now consider yourself stupid.

Over time, this negative self-esteem lowers the quality of your life. You feel emotionally fatigued to the point where you feel less than others around you. You settle in your job, in the partner you choose, in the way you live your life because you're afraid. You might also find yourself in a place of being hard on yourself. You may start hurting and harming yourself with comfort foods, drugs, or alcohol to numb the pain and suffering that arises from the internalization of negative messages like: "I'm stupid." You might hurt and harm yourself through isolation, for example, by dropping out of school or deciding not to go at all. You might not ask for a well-deserved raise, fearing that your supervisor thinks you are stupid and unworthy. If we personalize our roles in life, it can lead us to our own demise.

## SINKING INTO LOW SELF-ESTEEM

You sink into a place of low self-esteem by believing things that are not true. Until you record over the negative *I'm stupid* message, you will settle for less, and lack the confidence to pursue your dreams and interests over fears that you are not smart enough or good enough.

## GOING DEEPER

When we personalize the roles we play, they can cause us a lot of pain and suffering. If we can recognize that we are not the roles we play — and that we are in fact much more than that — we can learn how to stop internalizing the pain that has occurred while playing these roles.

For example, as a student, I studied hard and wrote a lot of exams, and I usually did pretty well. But on one occasion, I failed a multiple-choice exam. I knew that I had worked hard in class and understood and studied the material. Since the failing mark would show up on my university record, I asked the professor if I could rewrite the exam. She said: "You're a hard-working student, come back tomorrow morning for a rewrite." I went home and reviewed and then tried to get a good night's rest. The next morning, the prof gave me a written rather than a multiple-choice exam. This time I got 96 percent, which made me feel really good. This experience taught me that even though I understood the material, I struggled with the multiple-choice exam format. I wasn't stupid. I was better able to demonstrate my grasp of the subject matter in the context of a written exam over multiple choice.

## BUT WHAT IF?

What if rather than ask my professor for a rewrite that day I'd simply accepted my failing grade and assumed I was a failure and too stupid to pursue my academic goals? This choice could have had a catastrophic effect on my career and my future. I might have told myself that I was not smart enough or as worthy or capable as others. With that thought in mind, I would have had little courage with which to challenge my low self-esteem. I might have taken any job I could find rather than continuing my education, and thus lowered my quality of life.

I wanted to be a psychologist, but I wouldn't have been able to if I had given up. I would have become emotionally fatigued and compared myself to other people. I would have seen only that everyone else was doing better than I. I might have settled in life because of one poor grade on an exam, and I would have been hard on myself. I might have punished myself, and sought comfort in drugs, comfort foods, or alcohol to numb my pain and suffering.

Today, because of one failing mark, I could be merely existing rather than enjoying my occupation and living the full and interesting life I envisioned for myself. Because I had enough self-esteem, I found the courage to ask for a second chance. I rewrote and passed that exam, and my life took me on a positive course.

## UPS AND DOWNS

We experience all sorts of ups and downs over the course of a lifetime. If you lose a job, for example, why do you get depressed? After all, you are more than your job. Losing a job is an isolated event, not a never-ending pattern. If you regularly fail math exams, maybe math is not your forte. But when we take an isolated event, one person's criticism, or one break-up to heart and hold onto it, we fail to challenge ourselves to examine the possibility that it is not an irrefutable truth, but perhaps an isolated event.

## ISOLATED EVENTS VERSUS REPEATING PATTERNS

Let's talk about relationships. When we have a break-up, why do we often feel like we're never going to meet someone new? One break-up is an isolated event, not a repeating pattern.

We often connect with others on a soul level, but, for any number of reasons, sometimes we cannot sustain a relationship with someone over time. If you're a professional with set working hours who needs a lot of quiet time and you connect with someone who wants to party like a rock star, even if they are a great person and their heart is in the right place, chances are that relationship will not last. One of you is out there all the time, socializing, and perhaps burning the candle at both ends, while the other prefers a quieter, more introspective, balanced lifestyle.

For example, if you prefer to stay home in the evenings, watch movies, and snuggle, and your partner one day says: "I'm out of here, you're a drag. You're not worth being with," does that make you an unworthy person? No, it does not. But if you were to hold onto that person's assessment as the gospel truth, you might never get into another relationship. You might choose instead to isolate, to hurt, and harm yourself by self-soothing with alcohol, drugs, comfort foods, or other harmful behaviors.

Here's the key: an isolated event is not a never-ending pattern. When we get thrown off course by a job loss, we must realize that we are not just one lost job. We are more than that! When we break up with a partner, we need to remember that we are not simply a partner, we are much more than that.

Let's look at some remarkable examples. Helen Keller was much more than her lack of sight. Terry Fox was much more than an amputee. Nelson Mandela was much more than a victim of apartheid. Mahatma Gandhi's eldest son was an alcoholic who despised his father ... but Mahatma Gandhi was much more than a heartbroken, estranged parent.

## WE ARE MORE

Many of the most admired and accomplished people in the world have learned to recognize that they are more than their failures and shortcomings. We too are more. We are more than our depression, our anxiety, our ADD, our abuse, our failures, our childhood, our bank balance, our losses, our dysfunctions. We are more! We need to realize that we are not just the experiences and the roles we play in our lives. We are much more! We are at once perfect and a work in progress.

Just like children who live in the moment, we need to believe in the superheroes within us.

**In the exercise at the end of this chapter, you'll have an opportunity to explore the hurts you have personalized in your life: negative events and symptoms that prevent you from recognizing your true value and potential.**

We need to learn to rise above the negative events and messages we have accrued in our lives. I am not my anxiety. I am more than that. I am not my Attention Deficit Disorder. I am more than that. I am not my abuse. I am more than that. I am not my trauma. I am more than that. I am not my age and weight. I am more than that. I am not my relationship loss. I am more than that.

Self-worth does not come from just one area of our lives, nor is it defined, restrained, or diminished by isolated events. There is more to us! To love ourselves as we are, we need to have compassion for ourselves, our challenges, our pain, our struggles, and our suffering in the many roles we have played and are playing in our lives.

We have to recognize with child-like innocence that just because a couple of experiences have thrown us off, it doesn't mean that we are not good enough. We are, at once, perfect and a work in progress.

**In the exercise at the end of this chapter, you'll have a chance to reset your self-worth by acknowledging the negative events that have taken place in your life and taking inventory of your best qualities and attributes.**

You are worthy of love just the way you are. Learn how to love yourself, with your beauty and your scars, your traumas, and your hurts. Learn to strive to be better while recognizing that the obstacles and difficulties you'll encounter do not mean that you are not good enough.

We can strive to be higher, better versions of ourselves each and every day. That's our journey. Take a moment and practice the pause. Return to your notes from time to time, and review and add to your list of good things about you. Begin to appreciate your own worth just as you are. Reinforce this and one day you will truly align and feel able to believe it. Life is all about replacing one thought with another … replacing negative thoughts with positive, compassionate, supportive ones.

## EXERCISE

List the past hurts in your life that you have personalized.

What negative events, such as break-ups, job losses, and symptoms from your genetic make-up, have you internalized? Identify the hurts that keep you stuck and prevent you from recognizing your true value.

Make a list of the good things about you, your strengths, skills, patience, courage, dedication, persistence, and kindness. Don't be stingy. Go all out and be proud of every good thing about you!

_____

_____

_____

_____

_____

_____

_____

_____

_____

_____

_____

_____

_____

_____

_____

_____

_____

_____

# CHAPTER 15
# OBSTACLES AS LESSONS

Life, as I have said before, is just a series of experiences. We judge these experiences as positive or negative. The experiences we judge as negative tend to be those that inconvenience us. From day to day, what may inconvenience us can shift and change.

For example, a child asks his mother: "Please come upstairs with me. The boogieman is up there and I'm afraid to go alone." If his mother has plenty of time and no pressing demands, she may find the request cute and charming, and enjoy a trip upstairs to scare away the boogieman. But if this request coincides with a day the mother is juggling completing a work assignment while making dinner and doing laundry, the trip upstairs to banish the boogieman becomes a negative experience.

We need to start removing the 'positive' and 'negative' labels from our experiences. We need to begin looking at our obstacles and challenges in life as lessons, or as a pause where we can choose to do something different. Life only gives us what we can handle. Know that you can handle problems as they arise.

## PAUSES AND FLOWS

Let's talk about pauses and flows. When things are going pretty much according to plan, we see our life flowing as it should, without obstacles or difficulties. But when there are pauses — things that we don't expect that slow us down or throw us off course, such as illnesses, obstacles, or decisions we need to make — these pauses feel uncomfortable because they throw us off our pace. Having to pick up a sick child from school, or fix a flat tire, or nurse a nasty head cold may not be a big deal, but these things interrupt our flow, that is to say, the smooth predictability of our daily routines.

We need to start removing negative labels. Our fears say: *I don't know if I can handle that.* It's our job to make our faith that life doesn't give us more than we can handle bigger than our fears. We can handle it all, good or bad. Bring it on!

## FAITH VERSUS FEAR

Faith is believing in your skillset and knowing that you can handle whatever comes your way. When things go off course, we become stressed because we fear that we might not have what it takes to deal with a situation: *Am I going to lose my job if I leave the office and pick up my sick kid for the third time this month?* or *I don't have time to deal with repairing my car.* We get stressed out about imagined catastrophic possibilities and worst-case scenarios. Fear is simply the absence of faith, a lack of faith in your ability to handle whatever challenges come your way. Let's start with that.

While everything in life is possible, we need to explore the probability of a worst-case scenario taking place. My boss might fire me for leaving to pick up my sick child from school. But how probable is it? I have a great track record at work. Everyone on my team loves working with me. I don't have emergencies like this often, and my child is really sick. If my boss doesn't have compassion for my situation, maybe this is not the right place for me.

## CHALLENGING OUR THOUGHTS

We need to start challenging the thoughts that we give weight to. Anything is possible; but what is probable? Say I've always feared that I would be hit by lightning: what is the probability that this is going to happen? It's not raining. I'm indoors. I live and work in a city full of tall buildings where my chances of being hit by lightning are even lower than most. We need to challenge our cognitive distortions, our inaccurate ways of seeing reality.

**In the exercise at the end of this chapter, you'll be asked to explore your thoughts and judgments about the challenges in your life.**

We need to recognize that in life we all have good days and bad days. On a good day, things flow a little bit smoother. On a bad day, they don't. You might need to slow down, take extra care, or change your agenda or expectations for the day. But it's not a big deal. Good days or bad, you can handle it.

Life only gives you what you can handle. To date, you've handled whatever has come your way. Reinforce your belief that you can handle whatever comes your way. Embrace everything that comes into your life as a lesson. Embrace every obstacle as a lesson for growth. Remove labels. And on challenging days, add in some self-care, have a treat, walk, chat with a friend, have a movie night or dinner out, engage in a hobby. Do something that brings you joy.

## OBSTACLES AND UNCERTAINTIES

Everything running smoothly for too long can leave you unprepared when obstacles and uncertainty pop up. Unexpected occurrences are not all bad: you could win the lottery. But even winning the lottery could bring unimagined challenges. You could get a better job, be offered a transfer or promotion; all good, but such opportunities come with obstacles and challenges of their own. We might initially be afraid of change or worry about stepping into a new role with added pressures and greater responsibilities.

For example, as my mother entered her final year in the workforce before retiring, her job shifted. She was assigned to a later shift with fewer working days. Initially, she was upset and perceived this change as negative and disrespectful of her long-time service to her employer. But in the fullness of time, her perception changed. She came to see these changes as invaluable because her revised work schedule prepared her for the transition into retirement.

We often judge the changes in our lives as negative, but these changes often show up for our own betterment. Remove judgment. Allow yourself the confidence to embrace things that come up in your path. Consider that they have shown up for your own betterment and growth.

When something happens to you, consider it a message. It is showing you something about yourself. After that, every time it repeats, it is a test. For example, the first time I experience a relationship becoming unpleasant and hurtful to me, I am being shown features or behaviors in another person that I find problematic. From then on, every time these same features or behaviors reappear in new relationships, I am being tested. Have I learned my lessons from the first person who hurt me? Am I just repeating my past mistakes, and choosing that misaligned 'bad boy' — or 'bad girl' — over and over again? Or am I able to change my patterns of behavior and make better choices for myself?

### THE SAME MISTAKES

While it is easy to see when friends make the same mistakes over and over again, we often do not recognize the repeated patterns in our own lives. So, in my first 'bad boy' relationship, I learned the lesson that this particular type of person is not a good fit for me as I strive to become my highest and best self. In my first failed career move, I learned that a certain type of job or setting or boss is not a good fit for my skills, interests, temperament, or goals. Life is trial and error. I accepted what didn't work and kept trying new experiences, and I allowed my growth to lead to a better fit for me.

After learning the valuable lessons gained by living through challenging situations, every time you're faced with an opportunity that falls into the same pattern, it's a test. Have you grown enough through your experiences to recognize a repeated pattern? Can you say to yourself: *I'm not doing this again; it doesn't work for me*? Can you stand up for yourself, be assertive and brave, and seek out what works for you, rather than repeating patterns and people pleasing or otherwise following the same path over and over? You can make a job or relationship work or fit, but our goal is to find our best possible fit.

You need to embrace your life experiences — including the negative ones — as a series of opportunities for growth, opportunities to learn lessons, opportunities that reveal aspects of yourself that you need to address, stay with, or move away from so that you can begin to set healthy boundaries for yourself.

**In the exercise at the end of this chapter, you'll have an opportunity to reflect on some of the most important 'hard' lessons you have learned, and how these lessons informed your choices moving forward.**

Yes, there have been and will be hard days. But you need to realize that on those days when you encounter pauses and obstacles, you're also being taught how to rest, how to be kind to and love yourself, how to bring in elements of self-care.

Self-care can be as simple as ordering dinner rather than dragging yourself, exhausted, off to the grocery store to shop for food, then heading to the kitchen to prepare a meal. It could mean canceling a night out with friends and just relaxing at home if you're feeling stressed and fatigued at the end of a challenging day. On difficult days, allow yourself the choice to slow down, and add in self-care. Realize that the fabric of life is learning and growing. Every obstacle has its place and purpose in your growth. If you accept it, you can roll with the punches, enjoy the good, and recognize and embrace the lessons of the obstacles. It's all part of life's journey.

## EXERCISE

We need to challenge our thoughts. Being a better, higher version of ourselves requires us to recognize our judgments and where we place our value. Tell your inner child that you deserve it all and nurture them with compassion to live life fully.

Ask yourself:

- Are you making the challenges in your life heavier than they need to be?
- Are you magnifying the probability of bad things happening?
- Do you tend to focus more on what is not working than what is in your life?

Think about the most important 'hard' lessons you have learned through challenging situations in your life. How did these lessons inform and influence your choices? Are you growing or feeling like a hamster on a wheel going nowhere.

# CHAPTER 16
# BECOMING A HIGHER VERSION OF YOURSELF

This chapter is all about becoming higher versions of ourselves. The chart below illustrates a cycle of life from childhood into midlife and beyond.

When we are growing up, we are sponges, we're eager, we're enthusiastic, we're in a place of learning and growth. There's a big world out there to explore, and we're itching to take it all in. It's all new! In our youth-obsessed culture, we celebrate and embrace this phase of life. But it's only just the beginning of a long, exciting journey.

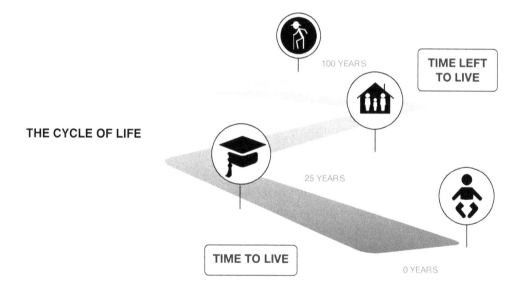

THE CYCLE OF LIFE

It's important to understand life's phases. In the first part of life, up to age 25, there is a lot of energy and enthusiasm. We're full of vigor and zest for life. Everything is a new experience. Newness in life creates interest. But life can be heavy in this *time-to-live* first phase. You don't have money, you're trying to go to school, trying to figure out what your career will be. You have many influencers pulling you away from your truth, telling you what they think you should do, who you should be, and how you should live your life. Your parents think you should be one thing, and society is showing you other options. Maybe you have attention/learning struggles or anxiety hindering you from performing at the level you know you are capable of. We struggle with a lot of things in this first phase of life. It's a tough time to live through.

We have a glorified image of youth. But as we mature beyond this phase, we begin to sense that life is fleeting and short. Often, in the second phase of life, between the ages of 35 and 55, we experience a midlife crisis.

## THE SECOND PHASE OF LIFE

In this second — *time-left-to-live* — phase of life, the responsibilities and challenges begin to mount. Our parents begin to age. Eventually, they get old and sick, and many times we become their caregivers. At the same time, we take on more responsibilities, such as raising children, servicing a mortgage, and meeting the increasing demands of a job. In this phase of life there is more sacrifice required of you. Life appears busier, more time-pressured, and stressful.

Also, there's more wear and tear on your body, and you lose interest in things that were once exciting and novel. You've been there and done that a thousand times, and what once gave you joy no longer holds your interest. Intimacy may decline, interest in established hobbies or activities might fade, and you might find yourself no longer excited about travel or activities that you once looked forward to with enthusiasm. You might also feel stress about long-term finances and the time looming in your life when you will no longer be able to support yourself in the same way. You might realize that you made decisions in your youth that are unfavorable for your older years.

## BECOMING A BETTER YOU

No matter what stage you're in, it is important to strive to become a better version of yourself. But what does this mean? A better version of the self is not about accomplishment. We're taught from an early age to strive to achieve success and make something of ourselves. But where are we going? And why so fast? What's the rush? We're often trying so hard to accomplish and arrive that we fail to bring in self-care and self-love. If you push too much and work too long and hard, you just might peter out earlier than you otherwise would. True success in life includes quality self-care rather than always putting the needs of others ahead of your own. It is smart to reflect. Ask yourself, *if I died today how would people remember me?* Are you living a quality life that people would appreciate and reflect back on with respect at your funeral?

We go through life thinking of happiness as a destination, a point in the distant future when at last we will have achieved and accumulated all that we want. We think we will be happy when we finish school. When we finish school, we think we will be happy when we get married. Once we're married, we think we'll be happy when we have children or a better job, more financial security, a better car, a better home. Then one day, we die, still waiting to be happy.

## NOT A DESTINATION

Life is not a destination. It's a journey. It's about living each and every day, every moment in your truth. Are you living each day fully with joy and pleasure? Are you sparking interest? Are you learning how to incorporate self-love and self-care into your life? Are you able to live each day as if it were your last?

It's important when striving to be a better version of yourself to step back from the cycle of being well-adjusted to a sick society. A sick society promotes overworking, over-stretching, getting caught up in superficial material acquisitions, sacrificing yourself for others all the time, burning out, being sick, losing your sense of purpose and joy in your own life, and not taking care of your relationships or your mind, body and soul.

In your final hours, you're not going to be fretting about not spending enough time working, you are going to agonize over time and energies not spent enjoying your life, interests, and relationships with others. Your colleagues, clients, and professional connections will not be by your side in the end, but the people you sacrificed will be there. Are you living a life aligned with how you want to be remembered?

A person striving to become a better version of themselves goes beyond their habits, daily routines and responsibilities and really looks at their self-evolution. The higher version of yourself goes beyond the daily routines and responsibilities and asks: *What is my self-evolution?*

We often become depressed when we put so much pressure on ourselves. We stay isolated and stuck in a place of loneliness. But when we strive to be a higher version of ourselves, we constantly work on our mind, body, and soul, on our relationships with and our service to others, on relations with family and friends and our community.

Without self-love, self-care, and self-fulfillment, we are truly alone. We don't make time to be healthier. We don't make time for our minds to be healthier. We don't challenge our negative thoughts and we don't engage in meaningful, in-depth conversations with others. We get stuck in superficial chit-chat, caught up in superficial comparisons. We often feel empty, even after spending time with people we care about. This void is a sign that we need to work on ourselves and our life on a deeper level.

## THE WELL OF DEPRESSION

When people are suffering from depression, they feel hopeless about life and trapped as if they were at the bottom of a well. When you're stuck in a well of depression, you feel alone, out of place, disconnected, unable to relate to others. You feel cold, lonely, confused, disheartened, and lost. Even if you're surrounded by people and beauty, you feel disconnected from everything good and sustaining.

Emerging out of depression is like climbing out of a deep, dark well. We need to learn how to embolden ourselves to look up from the well and see a point of light. That light is the hope that you can climb out of the dark place. You have the skillset to do it no matter how stuck you feel. This hope musters up a little bit of energy that allows you to begin to wedge your hands and feet into the cracks and grooves in the walls to raise yourself up. You can do it. As humans, we are made for survival. Our bodies do everything to survive threats. We just need to align with and trust ourselves.

## OUT OF THE WELL

Step by step you rise higher and higher. Not wanting to return to the darkness, you don't look back. You keep climbing higher, searching in the darkness for the next opportunity to grab onto. Finally, you reach the edge of the well, and you pull yourself out. You are warmly welcomed by a ray of sunshine. Sunshine brings you connection, hope for a better moment. You feel the warmth of the sun and the healing light on your face. The wear and tear on your body and soul from the darkness of the well melts away as the sun invigorates your body. Visualize reaching out and grabbing a piece of that sun and putting it in your heart. Now your heart radiates this beautiful light. This light spreads from the top of your head down to the tip of your toes. It brings you to a place of healing from within.

In depression, we allow our mind, body, and soul to stay connected to negative ruminations, darkness, and pessimism. We put ourselves deeper and deeper into these wells. If we don't find a way to see hope and light, to pull ourselves out, we can feel alone and disconnected, which can lead to pain and suffering. We can get to the point of wanting to leave this life.

## RECREATING INTEREST

Buddhist teachings say that we must constantly strive to recreate interest in and passion for life. In the first phase of life, there is so much to be interested in. We're young and the world is waiting for us to explore. But as we get older, it's harder to create interest because we have been there and done that on so many fronts.

**In the exercise at the end of this chapter, you'll have a chance to examine your current life phase and take inventory of your daily positive practices. And you'll be challenged to imagine ways of bringing more joy and excitement into your life.**

## YOUR LIFE'S WORK

Becoming a higher version of yourself means thinking positively, seeing the light, having more faith than fear, and constantly working on yourself. Being alive in health takes work, care, and attention. We need to start paying attention to our mind, body, and soul and to our relationships with friends, family, co-workers, and our community. (When I refer to the 'soul,' I am talking about a spiritual connection to our own spirit, truly enjoying your own company.) When you are alone, do you enjoy your own company or are you exhausted? Do you like what goes through your mind? Are you ruminating negative, racing thoughts? Are you at peace with yourself? Do you feel happy and appreciate where you are, or are you constantly looking to be elsewhere? Do you have negative memories, sadness, loneliness, fears, self-dislike, doubt, and anxiety?

You enjoying your soul — enjoying your self-esteem and taking pride in who you are — seeing the qualities you were born with, the positivity, the happiness, the unconditional love, the vigor for life, your ability to speak your truth, and living on your own terms, as children do, is possible at any age.

You are not your age. You're more than that! Recognize that to be a higher version of yourself, you need to work on yourself every day, climb out of the well when you need to, to find vigor and light in your life. Bring in happiness through gratitude and recognize positivity, eating well, exercising, and limiting or eliminating alcohol and drugs that could be depressing you. We need to be kind to ourselves. We often bring substances into our lives that can cause depression and anxiety. Alcohol, for example, is a depressant. It depresses the central nervous system and is not aligned with lifting us up when we are already in a low place.

Begin to explore what you put not only in your body but also in your mind. In the exercise at the end of this chapter, you'll explore difficult questions, including how hard you are on yourself, how negative your thoughts are, what cycles through your mind as lingering, unfinished business, and other questions.

The goal here is to start challenging yourself, no matter what stage of life you're in. Establish goals for yourself and bring in baby steps to get you started on your way. Acknowledge and celebrate your minor gains as big wins. If you're eating well and exercising, if you've stopped scrutinizing and criticizing your appearance, and you're working to align yourself with your vision of a healthier version of yourself, you are on your way. Everything will fall into place over time. Living healthy is a choice we need to make — over and over — for our betterment.

Have compassion for yourself. Things take time. Have compassion for your genetics, your stage of life, and for how stressful life can be. Set an intention to become a better, higher version of yourself.

## EXERCISE

Whatever age you're at right now, take a look at your day-to-day life. Whether you're in a time-to-live or time-left-to-live phase, ask yourself the following questions:

- Are you living with vigor?
- Are you embracing your life with happiness?
- Are you bringing in moments of self-joy, self-love, compassion, and connection with people you care about?
- Are you celebrating life, or just going through the motions?
- Do you look forward to the day ahead every day?

_____

_____

_____

_____

_____

_____

_____

_____

Explore what you put in your mind:

- How hard are you on yourself?
- How negative are your thoughts?
- What goes on in your mind that feels like lingering, unfinished business?
- What do you hold on to, that no longer serves you?
- Are there hurts in life that you are still stuck on?
- Are you happy with the relationships in your life or do you need to make more connections and deepen the ones you have with the people in your life?
- Are you living your life on your terms or are you afraid?

Make note of any issues that come up.

_____

_____

_____

_____

_____

_____

_____

_____

_____

_____

_____

_____

_____

_____

_____

_____

_____

_____

_____

_____

_____

_____

_____

Take a moment right now to set an intention of becoming a better, higher version of yourself.

# CHAPTER 17
# YOUR AUTHENTIC SELF

We're born playful, innocent, feeling like superheroes, in a state of unconditional love. As children, we embody magnificent energy, passion, and presence. We live each moment in positivity, high self-esteem, and connectedness. This is our authentic self — the one that we are born into.

Over time we start losing and letting go of our connection to our authentic self. We replace much of that positivity and vigor with low self-esteem, self-criticism, and fear. We internalize hurtful things and feel afraid to re-experience pain, hurts, and struggles.

## STRIVING FOR AUTHENTICITY

Each and every day, we need to strive to bring in reminders of our authentic self, our true self, the one we were born with, in high self-esteem. We need to recognize that every one of us has a true, unique, authentic self. We are unique in our expression of ourselves, our interests, our passions.

Each and every one of us also has a battlefield inside. Our authentic selves struggle with what is expected of us. We need to learn to follow our truth and fight for our authenticity, for our greater good.

In this chapter, you will begin the challenge to reinvent yourself. You will begin to look at your life and take action to reinvent it for your own greater good.

## FACTORING YOUR AUTHENTIC SELF INTO YOUR LIFE

In previous chapters, we've talked about how when we are in pain (low self-esteem, anxious, doubtful, negative, depreciative, unhappy), we spill our pain onto others. When you work on yourself, you also spill positivity onto others. Don't give from your well, give from your overflow: an overflow of positivity, love, kindness, support, and compassion.

We make time to take on extra work, help others, or lend a hand when asked. It's time to start factoring yourself into your life. Start by setting aside time every week to strategize and plan ways to move toward becoming a more authentic, healthier, kinder version of yourself.

Children eat regularly, go to bed early, and get enough sleep. They rest when they need to, they reach out for affection when they need it, they follow their feelings, and seek out what they require to feel good and whole. As we age, we hesitate or feel embarrassed to share our needs, and we fear that people will not love us as we are. Where did the doubts creep in? Why are you holding onto them as absolute truths? We all want to be loved and accepted. We all just mirror and hesitate to reach out because of self-deprecating thoughts and isolated hurtful experiences or influences.

## THINK ABOUT IT

Imagine for a moment not that you are a child, but that like a child, you could seek out or ask for what you want or need. Think about your life. What would you like to change? Take a moment to recognize, in your mind, body, and soul, what concerns you about your relationships with your partner, family and friends, co-workers and your community, your finances, your career, and your health. Acknowledge the areas of positivity and prosperity and note the areas of your life where there is dysfunction caused by your own actions. Are there areas in your life of hurt, harm, ignorance, and avoidance that stem from your behaviors? Are there areas of concern where you could begin to take action?

Let's explore some ways you can begin today to connect with your authentic self.

## NOURISHMENT

Your relationship with food is a great place to start. I facilitated a group therapy program called *Food for Mood*. This group was all about facilitating understanding that when your mood is off, your food habits tend to go off track as well. When we're feeling sad, worried, depressed, or lonely, we crave comfort foods or withdraw from food altogether. When we're feeling happy and in control, we make healthier choices, in alignment with our wellbeing. When we're feeling sad, or victimized, or overwhelmed, or triggered by trauma, we crave numbing agents, such as drugs, alcohol, and comfort foods.

It's important to recognize what you put into your mouth, and the purpose it serves. Are you eating for nutrition and energy, or to deplete and numb yourself? Have you formed comfort habits from your upbringing? Did your mother offer food as comfort, or did you grow up in a culture centered around food rather than food as nourishment? Examine your relationship with food and mood and the patterns and habits you have formed.

## SELF-TALK

Another great starting point is how you start your day. We wake up in the morning and do not speak to ourselves with high self-esteem. We wake up and drag ourselves into work feeling tired. People ask us how we are, and we answer with the flat-line response: "Fine." We often criticize our weight, fatigue, age, or level of accomplishment in life.

We fail ourselves when we fail to look at ourselves positively. We might criticize the way our clothes fit. We put pressure on ourselves to look a certain way. At work, we feel like we're behind, or not up to the tasks at hand. We scrutinize and deride ourselves from the moment we wake up until we go to sleep at night. How is this in any way positive or healthy?

What would shift if you took the time to look at yourself and acknowledge your true self? Think what would change if you could say: *My true self is unconditionally loving, giving, caring, intelligent, funny, strong, powerful, cute, pretty, compassionate, handsome, loyal, accountable, trustworthy, generous, organized, patient, considerate, cooperative, fearless, worthy, knowledgeable, capable, creative, kind, artsy, beautiful, amazing, athletic, enthusiastic, self-loving, dependable, reliable, empathic, forgiving, grateful, friendly, helpful, honest, punctual, respectful, resourceful, understanding, pure, innocent, a good partner, a good parent, a good friend, a loving daughter or son, spiritual, driven, and vivacious.*

There are so many beautiful words we can use to describe ourselves. How do you speak about yourself? Self-talk is important.

## AFFIRMATIONS AND MANTRAS

Affirmations are a powerful means of aligning with your authentic self. Think of affirmations as a way of planting seeds for the future. The future, after all, is nothing more than the imagination. It could be positive or negative. Are you planting the seeds of positivity for your future, or are you planting seeds of fear, anxiety, and worst-case scenarios?

If the future is uncertain, it means you can make it as beautiful as you want it to be. You can plant any seed you want. Affirmations can help you plant the seed of what you want to bring into your life, what you want to manifest. Affirmations such as:

- *I bring in an abundance of money.*
- *I am safe, healthy and protected.*
- *I am capable.*
- *I bring in the love of my life.*
- *I bring in success.*
- *I work with ease.*
- *I bring in balance with ease.*
- *I am always in a state of love, gratitude, or calmness.*
- *I am worthy of love just as I am.*

## AFFIRMATIONS

Let's talk about how you speak to yourself in moments of stress. Are you able to pull yourself out of a negative state of mind? In moments of stress, you can use affirmations or mantras to pull yourself out of a negative state. Imagine saying to yourself in moments of doubt: *I am worthy of love just the way I am.* Imagine, when you're feeling vulnerable, saying: *Nothing bad leaves me. Nothing bad comes to me.* These affirmations can make you feel supported, positive, and protected in times of self-doubt.

You can use affirmations to reconnect with your authentic self, and support yourself when you're feeling less than, stressed, anxious, or vulnerable. Affirmations can replace negative thoughts in moments of anxiety and take you to a place of calmness and self-care.

**In the exercise at the end of this chapter, you'll have a chance to create affirmations of your own. You can use your affirmations to reconnect with your authentic self, and support yourself when you're feeling less than, stressed, anxious, or vulnerable.**

## SEED MANTRAS AND CONTEMPLATIVE MANTRAS

Mantras are very useful tools. They can replace negative thoughts in moments of anxiety and take you to a place of calmness and self-care. There are two types of mantras. *Seed mantras* are single words you can drop at any time, in silence. People often use a seed mantra to calm the mind. An example of a seed mantra: Love. Love. Love. Love. A *contemplative mantra* is a sentence or statement that you can repeat as often as you like to overpower your negative statements and empower yourself. Here's an example of a contemplative mantra: I am capable. I am capable. The Ho'oponopono Prayer is a popular Hawaiian healing mantra-like tool for facilitating forgiveness of others and self. The statements repeated are: "I am sorry. Please forgive me. I love you. Thank you."

By repeating these words or phrases in your head, you are reaffirming on a vibrational front where you want to be and how you want to feel, versus how you might be feeling in a moment of vulnerability or negativity. You can't have two thoughts working simultaneously, so replace negative thoughts or statements with positive ones. Take charge of the content repeating in your head. Your thoughts lead to your moods and physical symptoms, and consequently affect your actions and behaviors. So take charge of your thoughts.

## BREATHING

Breathing is a powerful way to reconnect with your authentic self. It's the quickest way to ground yourself and get out of your head. Often, when we are stressed, we take short and shallow breaths. When we are taking short and shallow breaths, we are not bringing enough oxygen into our bodies. This stresses our body and tightens our muscles. It is important to incorporate breathing as a means of bringing you back to yourself, grounding yourself, and reconnecting with your authenticity. The *box method* of breathing is simply a six-second inhale and six-second exhale. It is a powerful means of deep breathing that can ground you and calm you down. These deep breaths also bring sufficient oxygen into every part of your body. Proper oxygenation makes you feel healthier and more relaxed.

## KINDNESS

What you put out there will come back to you. Take a moment right now. Think of yourself as your highest self in your most authentic life. Just as when you're in pain you spill over onto others, when you are your authentic self, you spill over your joy and you will receive joy in return. When you act in kindness, you receive kindness back. When you give love, you receive love in return. Are you putting out there what you want to receive? Whether it's kindness, respect, compassion, or understanding, take a moment to identify and recognize what you put out all day long, and think about what you receive in return. Is it positive, negative, or neutral? Identify and recognize what you put out all day long, and think about what you receive in return. Is it positive, negative, or neutral?

**REST**

Rest means that you care about your body and your mind enough to put it in a place of rejuvenation and replenishment. Do you bring rest into your life? Do you bring in balance? As much as we want to conquer the world, get to the top and be ahead of our schedules, at some point, something's got to give. Some say that a well-kept home is an unlived life. It's okay to live with a little mess. Sometimes we need to relax and restore.

Give yourself permission to do things that bring you pleasure, enjoyment, fun, rest, and playfulness. Life is not all about responsibilities and things that have to get done.

Look at your life with a magnifying glass. Are you living your authentic life? Are you doing things that bring passion and interest into your life? Or are you doing things that are depleting you, that keep you merely existing rather than living?

Your authentic self is closer and more accessible than you think. Explore these and other ways to reconnect with your authentic self.

# EXERCISE

You can use these affirmations to reconnect with your authentic self and support yourself when you're feeling less than, stressed, anxious, or vulnerable. Mantras can replace negative thoughts in moments of anxiety and take you back to a place of calmness and self-care. Louise Hay has recorded many beautiful affirmations. You can use these affirmations as inspiration for creating mantras of your own.

Take a moment to come up with a few of your own affirmations.

_____

_____

_____

_____

_____

_____

_____

_____

_____

_____

You can use these affirmations to reconnect with your authentic self, and support yourself when you're feeling less than, stressed, anxious, or vulnerable. Your tailor-made affirmations can replace negative thoughts in moments of anxiety and take you back to a place of calmness and self-care.

Create a seed mantra, one word you drop in silence to bring calmness, grounding, positivity, or gratitude/happiness. For example, Love, Love, Love or Om, Om, Om or Protected, Protected, Protected or Safe, Safe, Safe.

_____

_____

---

Create a contemplative mantra, a statement that reinforces something positive in you. Some examples: I am capable. I am safe, healthy, protected. My loved ones are well. I am worthy of love just the way I am.

---

# CHAPTER 18
# FLOW

Where your attention goes, your energy flows!

Throughout this book, we've worked on setting life goals. A goal is the beginning of a plan to move ahead toward betterment. You have to plan to manifest what you want in life. Good health is something you can plan for. Letting go of past hurts and trauma, forgiving yourself and others, improving family, peer, and work relationships, finding a more fulfilling job, or making a change in your career are all things you can plan to bring into your life. Set goals to become a higher, more authentic version of yourself. Everything you want, or intend to bring into your life, you can manifest.

In this chapter, we're going to explore attention, energy, and flow. You need to start recognizing that your mind is quite powerful. It can uplift you or lead to your demise. What we pay attention to is very important. You need to look at where your mind goes because that is where your energy is going to flow. Slow down, pause, and reflect to shift positively.

## PLANTING THE SEEDS

Planning is planting the seed of where you want to go. We need to pay attention to ourselves and what we want to bring into our life. We need to list our goals and create a vision for where we want to be in life, and turn our attention to things that will encourage success and bring forth the changes we want to make.

Make a weekly date with yourself to check in with your goals and your commitment to becoming a higher version of yourself. Pay attention to and make note of the obstacles and struggles that hold you back from achieving the goals you've set for yourself. This is crucial to moving forward in a healthy direction.

Accountability is important. It's important to be accountable to someone. Being accountable only to ourselves is great in theory, but we often let ourselves down and put ourselves last on our list of priorities. Bringing in supports to help achieve the goals you set is critical. Make note of the people who can act as your cheerleaders and those who will keep you accountable. Consider establishing a buddy system in which you and a friend act as support for one another. Sign up with a group that can help you reach your goals.

For example, if your goal is to take up running to get into shape, rather than doing it alone, you could find a group that helps guide novice runners into the sport knowledge-ably, safely, and with a sense of comradery. Rather than become discouraged because you are pushing yourself too hard, too fast, or in the wrong way, you will be more likely to achieve your goal surrounded by others who share your intentions.

Your weekly self-date check-ins could be supported by your partner or a friend going with you to a coffee shop where you will silently examine your goals and review your progress and obstacles in the supportive presence of another, and then share your progress with one another. Here, you can build accountability, authenticity, and a deep support system.

I'd like to share with you the story of how my own buddy system began. Michelle and I had been ordained together as ministers in the same spiritualist church. Over time, we kept meeting while studying meditation and teaching practices. Our connection in classes was strong and immediate. Years later, we reconnected over social media, and spoke over Skype to catch up. Realizing that we shared similar goals, we decided to check in with each other once every two weeks to provide support and accountability for the meditation goals we set for ourselves.

As we live in separate cities, we began bi-weekly meetings over Skype. We have been do-ing this for years, and I look forward and value our check-ins. We've also traveled to visit one another in person. We poke fun at one another, we share our failures and our success-es. We talk about the wobbles that throw us off course and keep one another inspired and on track. We send each other food logs and talk about what we will be working on in the coming weeks and months. We work on mind, body, soul, relationships, meal preparation, self-love, meditation, and many other goals we set for ourselves.

Commit to yourself, and when you find your support person, to them as well. Having friends who align with your goals makes your friendships a little deeper and more real. You won't be talking about shopping, vacations, and other superficial things. You'll be sharing what you've struggled with, accomplished, and learned, as well as your experi-ences, your goals, and dreams, forging a deeper, more fulfilling connection. You will help one another grow and be better, more authentic versions of yourselves. You learn from others who share their goals, and their goals may inspire you in some way too!

It is fascinating how beautiful life is when you have people in your life with whom you share similar goals. We're all interconnected. The food we eat sacrifices itself for our nourishment and life.

## TAKE A MOMENT

Take a moment. Create a vision board. People who are anxious and depressed have sometimes been carrying such patterns for so long that they don't know how to feel without them. So we not only need to imagine the way we want to be, we have to try to connect to the feelings that align with the healthier version of ourselves.

Create your ideal list and vision board, and imagine and connect to the feelings that come with that life being created. Imagine feeling the way you want to be. Try and break the pattern of feeling that what you have always carried needs to continue to be carried into today and every day after.

## TAKE SMALL STEPS

Take a look at your self-talk. I want you to look at where you are and plant the seeds of where you want to be. I'd like you to look at your ideal life. Without putting undue pressure on yourself, begin to take small steps that move you from where you are now to where you want to be. Everything does not have to change overnight. Change is a process. Achieving a goal is a process. Bring in people to help you work through obstacles in your way. Your supports can help you through times of self-criticism and the days that you wobble and go off course.

Look where your energy goes. Are you putting your energy toward things that are going to facilitate success in your life? Or are you putting your energies into things that are going to sabotage, distract, and hold you back from achieving your goals?

You need to love yourself, and believe in yourself. It's a choice. We can make this choice. We can learn to love and value ourselves. We can learn to strive to be in alliance with our own wellbeing and goals.

Being healthy in mind, body, and spirit doesn't just happen. It's hard work, recognizing and revising unhealthy habits. But it's worth it because it is what will get you closer to the life that you want for yourself.

You will age better and carry less of what does not serve your health and betterment.

You deserve it. Feel deserving of love just the way you are. Feel deserving of health and of the life you really want. Bring in supports to provide consistency and accountability to help you succeed in breaking bad habits and routines.

Have compassion for yourself on your journey. Things take time. You have a whole lifetime to reach your goals. Each and every day, love yourself enough to do at least one kind thing that aligns with you becoming a higher, better version of yourself. Be the hero in your own life. Show up and stand up for yourself. Be better, for yourself and others.

You're worthy of love just the way you are. Working on yourself is all about becoming a better, higher version of yourself. If there is a purpose to life, it is this.

Life is just a series of experiences. Through these experiences, as we learn more and more, we can strive to become better versions of ourselves. On tough days, when it is hard, treat yourself with compassion. Be gentle with yourself.

When life is flowing well, challenge yourself to take it up a notch. Commit to a bigger goal. Push yourself a little harder. In Buddhism, they say we need to constantly create interest in life so that we do not get depressed. Striving for a higher, better self is a goal that creates interest and betterment.

Strive to live in a state of wellness each and every day, in a state of positivity each and every moment. If you find that you spend most of your day in negativity, begin by intentionally, consciously bringing in positive thoughts several times a day. Whether through meditating, listening to a guided meditation, using deep breathing to ground yourself, bring in positivity. Break for a healthy treat, catch the scent of something pleasant, prepare yourself a delicious meal, repeat a mantra that makes you feel empowered and positive, commit to a goal, work through social anxiety, interrupt the cycle of negativity.

Start setting goals. Find hobbies and pursue interests that make you a better version of yourself. Take a break from the high standards and pressures you place on yourself. Most of all, love yourself. Make a start.

**CONGRATULATIONS!**

Congratulations for doing the work, completing this program, and for committing to making positive changes that will help you transform into a better version of yourself. This is what true happiness is. It's a choice. It's you choosing to be better.

Decide to heal. Decide to love. Decide to try. Decide to replace negative thoughts with positive ones. As you heal past hurts and begin to thrive and grow, you give others permission to do the same. Set a shining example. Decide to connect. Decide to help yourself, to be kind, to sit with whatever shows up. Decide to set yourself free of pain, and to forgive. Decide to embrace gratitude. Decide to be the version of you that you truly long to be. Decide to create space in your life for moments of joy and gratitude.

Choose to accept yourself as you are. Celebrate your progress. And continue to set goals to be a better version of you. We all wobble, and that's okay. Have compassion for yourself. You are both perfect and a work in progress. Own it! Own who you are, just as you are, right now.

Pay attention to your thoughts. Examine them. High levels of positive thoughts mean that you are aligned with your highest and best self. Watch out for negative thoughts that you don't agree with but affect you anyway. Guilt, jealousy, and parental values you may disagree with: these are the thoughts and feelings that are not aligned with your highest and best self.

This is the beginning of your journey of choosing to live your best life.

Revisit the chapters and exercises in this book from time to time. Review the goals and strategies you've set for yourself. Reenergize and renew your commitment to becoming your highest and best self.

It's time to make your faith bigger than your fear. Remember, faith is believing in your-self and your ability to change. And fear is self-doubt. It's you doubting your ability to handle things, to adapt and change. Making your faith bigger than your fear aligns with you living a better, more authentic, and happier life.

It's time to stop existing and start living!

# EPILOGUE

We all have takeaways from our life events and experiences. We are all survivors in our own way. We often take away what pertains to our issues or needs at that particular point in time. There is always a reason or a lesson behind why we are feeling attached to a thought or concept.

People don't act on their thoughts; they act on their feelings about their thoughts. We need to learn how to create our own life, make it matter, factor ourselves into the equation of our life, and create the version of ourselves that we want to be, not the version we think we need to be to fit in. It's important to imagine our ideal self, and manifest it.

Remember you are worthy just the way you are.

## THOUGHTS, INCLUSIONS, AND EXCLUSIONS

We attach ourselves to thoughts that create moods and feelings, then act on them. That's right — our thoughts lead to our moods and behaviors. We also attach ourselves to thoughts of exclusion. Reinforcement of our exclusionary thoughts leads to behaviors such as self-isolation. Inclusionary thoughts reinforced propel us to manifest connection with others, for example, to feel like becoming part of a community, or seeking out and participating in activities with like-minded people. It is up to you what thought you pick to reinforce and how it looks and plays out in your life.

What kind of life are you creating for yourself? I challenge you to look at your life. Are you staying stuck versus healing? Are you staying lonely versus connecting? Are you staying distracted versus focusing?

What are you focusing on? Whatever you focus on expands. Your inner world equals your outer world.

I have people asking about ego. How do I get rid of my ego? What is ego? The ego separates you from your truth. Ego makes excuses for why you cannot change. By getting rid of the concept of who you think you are, you are removing ego and learning how to just be who you are versus who you think you need to be.

Help yourself heal today and try to see the good in yourself in your mind. Envision it. Embody it.

## CLEARING THE WAY WITH EMDR

Eye Movement Desensitization and Reprocessing, widely referred to as EMDR, is a process that facilitates the healing and clearing of trauma. We all have layers of trauma. You can clear memories that are associated with unpleasant, hurtful, traumatizing emotions. Your memories are in your past, which means that the events that gave rise to them cannot affect you today. It's happened. It's over. However, many of us carry an affect attached to that memory. This is actually what we work to clear in therapy, and what we need to clear to be free.

You can hold onto and think about memories from your past, but if there's affect attached to them, they are holding you back from living freely. Rather than seeing memory as a page in your book from your past, you're carrying it forth into your present. Traumas get locked in our nervous system, along with their original pictures, sounds, thoughts, and feelings.

EMDR unlocks the nervous system, allowing our minds and bodies to process the experience on a deeper level. In other words, bilateral stimulation helps process what we're still attached to. In this process, one's own brain does the healing as it is completely in control. Replaying memories, we can see what has been personalized, and clear the intensity of the emotions and hurts of a negative memory or experience, and revise and reframe negative concepts into more positive, helpful and adaptive statements.

## IN THE DRIVER'S SEAT

The reality is that you have always been in the driver's seat, in control. The thoughts and feelings we attach to our memories are ours. We might not have control over the incidents and suffering that happen in our life, but we have control over the thoughts and the way we interpret them, and the way we attach ourselves to concepts and beliefs. The key is you are in control of your own therapy in life. You need to make time for it. Make time for your connection, healing, and rest. Often, our exhaustion and fatigue are, in fact, emotional fatigue.

How much or how little you do is up to you. The courage to go into your stuff is about you being fed up with carrying painful experiences that no longer serve your highest and best self.

As children, we sometimes come up with defense mechanisms that serve us well in our young lives in a time of need. But as adults, we don't question and challenge whether these defense mechanisms are still serving us (working for us), or if they are hurting us.

As a child, you might have suppressed, avoided, denied, and just moved on as a way of coping. But as an adult, these mechanisms might no longer serve you. You might need to mature and realize that you are no longer a child in a household where you are stuck. You are an adult now and you can choose your life. This means you don't need to avoid things; rather, you can address them.

Our coping skills need to evolve throughout the various stages of our life. That's something many of us don't understand, and in therapy many times, this is what we are uncovering: better ways of coping when we're not in a place of survival or a place of threat.

Traumas of racism, abuse, physical pains, medical maltreatments, COVID, death, sudden life changes, bad news, shock, vulnerability, heartache, disappointment in ourselves or others — we carry pain as a reminder not to go through those experiences again.

We can grow and learn that we don't need to carry memories with the same level of hurt we felt when we first experienced them. This just holds us back. Instead, it's okay to have memories of incidents without the pain attached and have compassion for ourselves and what we've gone through and how painful it once was. Shifts in how we see ourselves are about us learning to be who we need to be: a happier, healthier version of ourselves.

## COPING WITH ALCOHOL AND DRUGS

Often, people cope with alcohol. Alcohol is often a gateway to the use of other drugs. Substances numb negative physical and emotional states. People who get into addictions have a lower pain threshold, a lack of tolerance for unmanaged stress, so learning to cope better, learning how to have better habits helps people disrupt the negative patterns in play. We sometimes 'use' to take a break from life, stresses, ruminations, racing minds, sadness, and feelings of low self-value.

So, once upon a time, if you did cope by using alcohol or drugs, today we can find a way to disrupt the habits in you and help you learn how to find a healthier way of coping with stress, with supports, resources, and healthier ways of being.

I often help people with the concepts of what holds us back — the stories, values, and belief systems that we take on. One that's very common is: *I'm not safe in my world*. I tell people to trace that concept back in time, to go to a target memory where once upon a time, they might have had a childhood experience where they felt unsafe in their world.

Sometimes we absorb our parents' fears and anxieties of not feeling safe in the world, and we take that on. Often, children born into immigrant families take on their parents' issues, anxieties, and perspectives of what the world should look like. Many of us take on our parents' anxieties, fears, money issues, relationship struggles, concepts of the roles of men and women, or racism.

Many times, we repeat patterns that have been projected onto us. Unthinkingly we end up reinforcing them and absorbing them on a cellular level; we repeat cycles and turn into our parents. Many of their fears and prejudices in turn become our own.

When you have a somatic symptom (a symptom that is experienced in the body), what words go along with it? This is important to look at. Many times when we have such experiences, it is good to go into them to discover the words that go with them, what associations go with them. Many times these words are holding us back.

## BRINGING IN RESOURCES

Installing positive resources is often what I do as a therapist. I try to help people recognize that they have the resources to cope with difficult things. Most of my work is helping people see that they have resources to help, support, and guide them through situations in which they feel a lack of nurturing, support, love, and capability. Our wise self, who is grown, can be of support when we truly feel alone.

I also try to help people imagine a positive future, envision where they want to be in life, with their issues, beliefs, and situations, versus being stuck in a situation and repeating patterns from the past.

Safety is established with resources. Install resources to feel empowered in life. Many people feel the child within. They see events and insecurities through a child's eyes and hold onto cognitive distortions, inaccurate ways of seeing reality. The adult self has a wiser mind and is more mature. Some of our adult cognitive distortions are very different from our childhood ones. We need to develop more realistic ways of seeing situations. We need to take time to realize how inaccurate our thoughts can be, and how we reinforce and keep cognitive distortions going that do not apply or make sense in our world today.

## BECOMING A UNITED FORCE

Let's try to connect the two worlds — that of your child and your adult — and close the gap, to unite the two. Using all aspects of yourself, restart and reconceptualize who you need to be, and become a united force. Hold your younger self's hand with compassion and let them know their adult counterpart can heal and grow beyond where they became stuck.

As children, we are perfect ... in high self-esteem, unconditionally loving. This is why we love children. They are full of love and compassion, living in their truth. They say it as it is. They have no filter. We love their innocence, purity, connectedness, and authenticity.

But as that child grows, they start attaching themselves to difficult, scary, horrible, or painful experiences. This begins a cycle where we become fragmented. We separate ourselves from our truth and start allowing these fragmented parts of ourselves to attach to stories that are not true: stories that are our parents' or symptoms of our parents. These are stories about how we're not good enough, we're not smart enough, we're not capable, we're damaged. This causes us pain.

In trauma, whether sexual abuse victims or victims of war, I find people often blame themselves: *It's my fault, I'm powerless, I'm damaged, I'm not good enough.* These are irrational beliefs that we give power to. Reinforced enough, they become, in a sense, a reality; they start to feel true to us.

We need to process pain and build a bridge to connect childhood experiences with the adult we are today. We need to take fragmented selves and make them whole again. We need to look realistically at our childhood and create a vision of who we want to be by merging our child with our adult and allowing ourselves to heal everything in the middle that we have acquired that no longer serves us or presents an accurate picture of our world as it really is today. Many of us are embarrassed about who we were. Rather than live in shame, embrace who you were, and see how far you have come.

We absorb our parents' insecurities, energies, judgments, belief systems, and values. We need to challenge ourselves and ask: *Are these values and beliefs mine? Do they work in my world for the life I want to create for myself?* We often claim values that worked for our parents' generation. But times change, and we too must change.

With childhood abuse, sometimes a child keeps going back to the abuser. It's not that they want to be abused over and over again. Many times, children go back seeking love, attention, and acceptance. It is not the abuse they are going back for.

Many times, as adults, they wonder what is wrong with them. *Why did I keep going back? Why didn't I speak up? Why didn't I seek help?* They often lack compassion for themselves as the child who went back seeking love, attention, acceptance, care, nurturing, or connection with someone they loved. Setting boundaries is a big part of our journey, but for abuse victims to work on boundaries, they need to understand where they left (abandoned) their boundaries.

We often yearn for comfort and attention and we put up with things in order to obtain it. We need to examine our imaginations and reimagine the ill thoughts that we've attached ourselves to, and we need to imagine adaptive, healthy statements for our betterment, self-protection, and highest good.

## CHALLENGING NEGATIVE THOUGHTS

We cannot blame ourselves for what happens to us. We need to look at how we are continuing the pattern today. How am I keeping it going in my life? We need to take accountability for revictimizing ourselves, day after day, by not revamping and not having compassion and love for the child who went through pain and suffering.

When you went out, did you know you were going to encounter abuse? When you went out, did you know you were going to have a car accident? Did you know you were going to go through a trauma? Did you know your father was going to pass away? We often harbor irrational statements in our heads, such as: *I shouldn't have gone out! Look what happened.* But when you went out, did you go out seeking abuse? Did you seek out trauma? No! We hold the irrational belief that we are in control of everything that happens to us. Therefore, we caused our abuse or trauma by choosing to go where we were assaulted, abused, or traumatized.

In my practice, I help people revise their thinking by challenging the negative and distorted thoughts that they hold onto out of habit or misconception. Many times we blame ourselves, not because we are blameworthy, but because it gives us a sense of control. A sense of a lack of control can make us scared of uncertainty and fearful of bad things happening at any time.

It's hard to live in a world with uncertainty. However, we are born into a world of uncertainty, and we do not know when and how we are going to die. We are born with uncertainty so we can become comfortable with it. We live in a society that teaches us to try hard to control each and every moment of our lives.

It's important to challenge our beliefs. Does everyone who does this get that result? Does everyone who goes out at night get attacked? Does everyone who gets into a car get into a car accident? We need to challenge ourselves to examine negative thoughts when we blame ourselves for negative things that happen to us. Did you know that if you went out that night, you would have a car accident? Typically, people say *no*. If we don't and can't know what is going to happen to us, how can we then blame ourselves? We didn't go out intending to cause ourselves harm. We didn't go to someone's home to be abused.

We need to recognize that we don't get into relationships hoping that we will be unloved or go through abuse. It is important for us to realize how we speak to ourselves, and how many times we speak to ourselves in a manner that is not in alignment with the truth. Remove the conditioning that hides your authentic, child-like self: your sense of love, compassion, belief, wonder, safety, and self-confidence — we were born with all of this. Where did we lose it?

## OUR INNER RESOURCES

We all have resources within us. Most of us are surviving, and yet we don't give ourselves credit for having survived difficult traumas in life. What does your child-self need to feel healed, safe, loved, protected, and able to deal with the world?

Start questioning yourself. As an adult, your inner child is still with you. What does that child need to heal? What does that child need to be a better version of themselves? What does that child need to feel more equipped to deal with society and not feel unsafe?

We have a universal connection to each other. We need to learn how to accept situations as they are and people as they are. And we all have choices amongst our acceptance. Our choices can liberate us from our pain. We can choose to let go of things, change things, and equip ourselves with better coping skills. The choice to carry pain is there, as is the choice to clear it.

Start again, right now. If you feel damaged, stressed, less than perfect, or a work in progress, that's okay. Start now. We're allowed to be 'perfect' and a work in progress at the same time. This is what is real. Things are as they are. Our painful experiences are incidents and events that we go through. And our brain can grab onto the associated concepts and thoughts to protect itself and survive, to help us through the painful, challenging experiences and protect us from them happening again. Our brain creates attachments to painful incidents, creates fear and self-doubt as a means to help us equip ourselves with better resources and coping skills.

It works in the moment, but if we hold onto these ill thoughts, we develop constricting beliefs, which hold us back and revictimize us. We stay stuck in the past rather than living our lives in the present.

An anxious child goes back and revictimizes him or herself constantly. Many anxious children have something akin to a loudspeaker in their bodies. Their symptoms are loud, and they constantly go to others to neutralize their energy and seek comfort. But they are abandoning themselves when they constantly look for other people to help them, leading to inner emptiness, a lack of sense of self.

Later in life, they need to learn to reintegrate themselves and know themselves better. As we learn we grow and develop aspirations, we seek out resources to better ourselves and our circumstances.

Using our emotions and our imagination, we can create health. After all, it is the imagination that holds onto ill health.

When an event happens, it's just that — an event. We judge events and link ill thoughts to them. These thoughts keep us stuck. It is our imagination that attaches negative thoughts, beliefs, and concepts to those experiences. The good news is that it is our thoughts that can liberate us and help us move forward from negative experiences.

## CREATING WHAT YOU NEED

In therapy, we work to create ideal supports (ideal parents, mentors, etc.). We bring in resources to feel empowered, so that we have a better life today, rather than staying stuck in trauma and revictimizing ourselves.

Create whatever you need! We have alter-ego states. We can create ourselves to be the person we want. Who is the person you want to be? If you're not the person you want to be, create a new persona, one who is more confident, who copes better, who feels empowered, and who feels worthy and deserving of good.

I see the emptiness in so many people, a feeling of lack, a feeling of void. You won't forget what has happened in your past, but with resources, you can shift, and you may even learn to grow. We don't replace our parents, but we can bring in new supports. At a time when you felt unsupported, you can imagine mentors — real people or people you create out of your imagination — helping you be a better version of yourself. I have a patient who chose to imagine Pocahontas as her support system, a person who played the part of a sibling helping her work through difficult times. (This patient had no siblings and her parents were in a troubled marriage.)

Many of us have confusion around compassion and responsibility. When we were growing up, our parents may have lacked supports. But as children we see our parents as omnipotent and omniscient. As adults, we can begin to accept that our parents were only human and that they were playing many other roles besides that of a parent. I ask people to imagine what their parents would have needed to be better parents when they were raising them. Sometimes it is possible for you to imagine good supports for your parents: to be healthier, better partners, and better parents, able to give you what you needed to feel supported and be a healthier child. This releases a child from feeling pressured to take care of their mother and father. We can bring in imaginary supports to teach our parents how to be better versions of themselves in our imaginations, removing the need for us to be their caretakers.

People ask: "What is imagination?" My simple way of explaining this is to ask how much they worry. And what do you worry about … about work, money, future, safety, your partner, love, loneliness? All the things you worry about … that's your imagination. Your worries are not real. You have created them in your imagination.

We can use our imagination to our advantage, for the positive. Rather than take a negative thought and reinforce it, we can light up a positive pathway and reinforce that through our imagination. When we open one door, it's like dominos, it links up to so many other doors. Negative pathways link to other negative pathways. What we focus on — whether it is positive or negative — expands.

When I do EMDR and I help someone look at *I'm not good enough* as a concept, what they will find is that their mind takes them to all the times they felt not good enough. Like dominos, it opens up all the memories, the times when they reinforced a negative pathway, the feeling of not being good enough.

In the same way, I can say that I am proud of myself. I am good enough. In the same way that a negative pathway opens, a positive one can open. Like dominos, you can end up with a bunch of memories that are positive, reinforcing how you are good enough, and how you can be proud of yourself.

Sometimes we hold onto pain because of fear. But if we let that story remain, then the person who caused us pain got away with it. And we will be susceptible to further hurts.

Who is suffering by holding onto these thoughts? I am. Is it worth it for me to hold onto negative thoughts and reinforce negativity in my life? When you let the negativity out of your system, the person who harmed you is not getting away with anything.

## RELEASING AND CLEARING

Past traumas are like movies you have playing over and over. You've seen it many, many times. In trauma, we reinforce our pain through flashbacks and nightmares. The key thing for people working through trauma to remember is that they survived it.

Add in resources and compassion for the suffering that you went through in your trauma and recognize and acknowledge that you survived the trauma. Resolve, strengthen, and reconceptualize life with gratitude, playfulness, compassion for the pain in the past, but with a new beginning for the current moment, where you are now. You have survived.

Abuse is confusing for children because they don't understand their attachment figures. Many times in abuse our attachment figures are our perpetrators. This is confusing because we are taught that safety comes with family, and strangers are the ones we have to worry about. But when family members cause us suffering through verbal, physical, or sexual abuse, we become confused about what is and is not safe.

## THE WORLD BECOMES A VERY FRIGHTENING PLACE

Negative constructs are learned and then reinforced. When we clear things, we allow ourselves to neutralize distorted ways of seeing reality, and we're left with compassion, love, and safety. Let's dissolve the conditions that we have placed on ourselves to feel unsafe, victimized, to feel hurt, and feel less than others, or not good enough. Let's look at our true selves and allow them to emerge.

We need to trust ourselves, to move past our pain, into a place of pleasure, compassion, love, and deservedness. In current situations with negative concepts, I ask, "When have you felt like this before?" Most often, whatever you're struggling with today connects to your past. Almost always, if you look backward, you will remember an earlier time when you felt like this.

Sometimes we do not recognize the patterns in our lives because the faces and details change. But when we take the time to examine our life stories, we can begin to see and understand our developmental history. A developmental history in therapy helps us discover important links and repeating patterns. In my private practice, becoming familiar with a patient's life story helps me see the repeating patterns in their life.

For example, if I have an issue with my father because he is a liar, maybe I move out. By moving out and distancing myself, I don't solve my problem, but I do avoid it. But then I end up having a roommate who is a liar. So I move out of that apartment because I don't want to be with a roommate who lies. Again, I don't solve my problem with liars, I simply distance myself from it, again, an avoidance maneuver. Now, I'm working at a place where my boss is a liar. I quit that job and move on because I am not good with liars. I'm still not solving my issue with liars; I am just separating myself. Now I find myself dating a liar, so I dump him. Next, I become a parent and find out my child is a liar.

**FACING YOUR ISSUES**

There are only so many times you can run away. Sooner or later you have to face your issues and learn how to deal with the people with whom you struggle. What in the past is linked to your behavior today? It is important to recognize this.

Addiction is linked to trauma. It's unprocessed neglect. Tease out blocking beliefs, negative cognitions that hold you back. Replace negative cognitions with positive ones. See the truth about your parents. They weren't capable of handling some situations and events, and that's okay. Learning how to see our parents in our truth not only humbles us, it gives us the power to forgive. Learning to see the truth of your parents' capacities showed you the truth of their limitations, their lack of capacity to be everything you needed them to be.

When you have a body sensation, it feels real. It's not just a thought — it's a thought with a feeling, and now there's a state attached. What is the belief that goes on in your mind that accompanies that feeling? Is that thought true? Or is it the feeling that makes it feel true?

Our job is to empower our inner advisor. We all have an inner advisor. We are all gifted enough to work through our pain. We want to heal. But we need to give it time and we have to stop numbing. We need to pause, reflect and breathe. When we slow down and breathe, we can respond in awareness and insight to heal and act with health and wellness in mind. Today's world of numbing with alcohol and drugs hurts us because we don't allow ourselves to heal, and what needs to heal is there, bubbling under the surface,

## EXAMINING POSITIVE AND NEGATIVE COGNITIONS

Let's examine positive and negative cognitions. It's important for us to recognize the core messages we say to ourselves. Here's a negative thought: *I did something wrong*. Reframing this thought could involve saying something to yourself along the lines of, *I've learned and I have grown from this experience*.

Here's a list of 'reframed' negative thoughts or cognitions:

- I don't deserve love.
  *I deserve love and I can have love.*
- I'm not safe.
  *I am safe now.*
- I am a failure.
  *I can succeed.*
- I am a bad person.
  *I am a good person.*
- I am broken.
  *I am beginning to heal.*
- I am worthless and inadequate.
  *I am worthy and enough.*
- I am not in control.
  *I am in control now.*
- I can't protect myself.
  *I can protect myself now.*
- I am stupid.
  *I have intelligence.*
- I have to be perfect.
  *I can be myself.*

- I am ugly.
  *I am fine and beautiful just as I am.*

Our thoughts are powerful. Remember, whatever we focus on expands. We need to learn to focus on more positives to bring in gratitude, appreciation, and sometimes even survival. Trust the wisdom within your body and build health. We can choose health. We choose unhealthy habits daily. But we weren't born with unhealthy habits.

We weren't born with a desire for alcohol. When we try it, at first it doesn't taste good, but we reinforce it over and over until it becomes desirable because we like its numbing effects. What are we numbing from? If you have a good life, you should be choosing to work through things, rather than numbing. If life is too stressful, take charge and change.

## PAST, PRESENT, FUTURE

Your past is your past. Your future is just your imagination. Start in the present, right where you are. Just be. Grace is a beautiful concept that indicates that life is orchestrated for our benefit, to grow and learn, and become the highest and best version of ourselves.

Our obstacles or patterns of overthinking and attaching ourselves to negative concepts and beliefs can become catalysts for change and growth. Master your life now and be a better version of yourself. Trust yourself to know that you can survive and navigate your way to where you want to be. If you want to be in success, love, healing, growth, and worthiness, you can do it. You just need to focus on bringing the supports and resources you need to be in that energy.

## CONNECT TO YOUR AUTHENTIC SELF

Your journey is to align with your authentic self. Never desert yourself. You are born alone. You die alone. Once here, you are interconnected to everything to help you be your highest and best if you choose to be. The journey is about you learning how to be a better version of yourself in the world in which you live. Imagine all your supports in alignment: healing reverses hurt; energy follows intention; love is the connecting energy. Connect to yourself and others and all around you.

Look at everything around you, the seen and unseen. Everything is holding you up. Everything is supporting you.

Trust yourself. Ask yourself: *What is the best next step for me?* Surround yourself with the supports that will get you to where you want to be. Take time to connect and renew yourself. Renew your mind, your body, and your soul. Ask yourself: *In suffering, am I running away from an old program or an old story? Am I stuck in an old pattern? Can I connect my current suffering back to the first time I felt this way? When have I felt like this before? When have I behaved like this before?*

Acknowledge old patterns, then return to the present and plant the intention of a new beginning. Allow your future to be what you want it to be rather than just a repeated pattern from your past. We don't need to reinforce expectations. We need to learn to live as who we are.

There are two reasons why we suffer in life — we don't accept people for who they are, and we don't accept situations as they are. Humble yourself. People don't have to live up to who you think they should be. They can be themselves. You need to look at how that person's actions affect you. If you have healthy boundaries, other people cannot affect you negatively.

## MANIFESTING THE LIFE YOU WANT

The steps you need to take to manifest the life you want are yours to take. Intention followed by action leads to a higher version of your life and yourself. Become one with the truth of who you need and want to be.

Our therapy comes from sharing our lives, becoming interconnected in the world in which we live. We need to learn how to feel supported, grow, and learn and acquire skills to facilitate a higher state of being. We are never alone in our pain. Trust me — we do not live alone. We are born alone, but we are born into families, systems, a society, with resources, in communities, in friendships, and in partnerships. We are never alone in our pain.

Sharing our sorrow halves it and sharing our happiness doubles it. Be real in your life and you will see that everyone shares aspects of your pain and issues. As we open up to our truth and our issues, we allow those around us to open up as well. In this way, we allow others to heal and rescue us, and help us to grow to be a better version of ourselves.

Envision where you want to be. Connect and align with your higher self. Take action. Outline what those steps will need to look like. Change comes through outlining and taking the steps to get there.

Bring in strategies and supports that will lead you to success. What might these supports look like? They could include mentors, buddy systems, therapy, coaching, parents, children, and more. Learn to surround yourself with people who are aligned with you being a better version of you.

## GIVING AND RECEIVING

Sometimes people lift us up, but sometimes people are unhappy with the changes we're making because our changes somehow negatively affect them. Say you're a giver. When you learn to step back and not give as much, the people who are used to receiving might not be happy with your change. But the people who have your best interests at heart will support you in the journey that you are on to become a higher version of yourself, even if it means they are not as much or as often on the receiving end of the relationship.

Learn to recognize your true allies, those who support the changes you are undertaking. And learn to see those who want to keep you stuck because it benefits them. Get pumped up. Align your energy to become motivated. There are a plethora of motivational speakers and empowering coaches out there. You might feel great after an uplifting talk, but that energy will soon fade unless you act on it. You need to do the work on your own to keep the energy and inspiration going.

## BEING YOUR OWN GOOD BOSS

Meditate. Go inward. Find affirmations that resonate within you. Create positive self-talk. Act and hold yourself accountable. Be your own good boss. Be laser-focused on eliminating your barriers, laser-focused on the baby steps you are taking, and laser-focused on where and who you want to be. Be clear with yourself that you deserve to be happier, healthier, and free of the ties that are holding you back. Consistency is key. Keep at it. To get the results, you need to keep going. Get into alignment with the positives in all areas of your life. Institute a daily practice. Hold yourself accountable and bring in the systems and supports you need.

People often ask me if they can change themselves and others. I say, of course. But you can only change others by first changing yourself. Motivate others to want to join you as you become a higher and better version of yourself. See the positives in yourself, and as you make gains, envision a larger picture with others changing around you.

As you change you might lose some people who are not ready or do not want to change. That's okay. As you grow you will attract new people.

The two things that affect us are our beliefs and our values. Change is about removing limiting beliefs and values. Learn to shift and see the truth. Free yourself of what no longer serves you. Pause, acknowledge, and release. Release, revise, reframe, and heal all that does not serve you. Learn to shift.

Most importantly, never disconnect from yourself. Every breath we take connects us to ourselves. Align with that breath. Every day we learn and grow. Release yourself from your victimhood. Your journey to freedom is you choosing to live in your highest and best self in every moment of every day. Call in your ideal self. Imagine it. Feel it. Know it. Manifest it.

It's time to stop existing and start living!

CPSIA information can be obtained
at www.ICGtesting.com
Printed in the USA
BVHW010622190422
634650BV00002B/4

9 781777 915506